D1709242

Creating Your Teaching Portfolio

Presenting Your Professional Best

Patricia L. Rieman
Northern Illinois University

Jeanne Okrasinski
Northern Illinois University

Mc Graw Hill **Higher Education**

Boston   Burr Ridge, IL   Dubuque, IA   Madison, WI   New York   San Francisco   St. Louis
Bangkok   Bogotá   Caracas   Kuala Lumpur   Lisbon   London   Madrid   Mexico City
Milan   Montreal   New Delhi   Santiago   Seoul   Singapore   Sydney   Taipei   Toronto

This book is dedicated to all the educators—preservice, inservice, and retired—who have been sources of inspiration for us throughout our lives. We thank you for being there.

Higher Education

CREATING YOUR TEACHING PORTFOLIO: PRESENTING YOUR PROFESSIONAL BEST

Published by McGraw-Hill, a business unit of The McGraw-Hill Companies, Inc., 1221 Avenue of the Americas, New York, NY, 10020. Copyright © 2007, 2000 by The McGraw-Hill Companies, Inc. All rights reserved. No part of this publication may be reproduced or distributed in any form or by any means, or stored in a database or retrieval system, without the prior written consent of The McGraw-Hill Companies, Inc., including, but not limited to, in any network or other electronic storage or transmission, or broadcast for distance learning.
Some ancillaries, including electronic and print components, may not be available to customers outside the United States.

This book is printed on acid-free paper.

1 2 3 4 5 6 7 8 9 0 QPD/QPD 0 9 8 7 6

ISBN: 978-0-07-287684-0
MHID: 0-07-287684-0

Vice President and Editor-in-Chief: *Emily Barrosse*
Publisher: *Beth Mejia*
Senior Sponsoring Editor: *Allison McNamara*
Editorial Coordinator: *Emily Pecora*
Executive Marketing Manager: *Sharon Loeb*
Managing Editor: *Jean Dal Porto*
Project Manager: *Margaret H. Leslie*
Art Director: *Jeanne Schreiber*
Designer: *Marianna Kinigakis*
Senior Production Supervisor: *Carol A. Bielski*
Composition: *10/12 Palatino, by Techbooks*
Printing: *45# Scholarly Matte Plus Recycled, Quebecor World*

Library of Congress Cataloging-in-Publication Data

Rieman, Patricia L.
   Creating your teaching portfolio : presenting your personal best/
Patricia L. Rieman, Jeanne Okrasinski. -- 2nd ed.
      p. cm.
   Updated edition of: Teaching portfolios, 2000.
   Includes bibliographical references and index.
   ISBN-13: 978-0-07-287684-0 (softcover : alk. paper)
   ISBN-10: 0-07-287684-0 (softcover : alk. paper)
   1. Portfolios in education. 2. Teachers--Rating of. I. Rieman,
Patricia L. Teaching portfolios. II. Okrasinski, Jeanne. III. Title.
LB1029.P67R54 2007
371.14'4--dc22
                              2006018888

The Internet addresses listed in the text were accurate at the time of publication. The inclusion of a Web site does not indicate an endorsement by the authors or McGraw-Hill, and McGraw-Hill does not guarantee the accuracy of the information presented at these sites.

www.mhhe.com

Contents

Preface

Originally published in 2000 as an ancillary "perk" with another college text, *Creating Your Teaching Portfolio: Presenting Your Professional Best* was so well received that McGraw-Hill sales representatives decided to make it available on its own. In this newly titled second edition, Rieman is joined by her colleague, Jeanne Okrasinski, as co-author. Rieman and Okrasinski stress the practicality of using a portfolio and the simplicity of its creation. The focus of this text is not limited to a single type of portfolio; rather, examples of various types and styles are included. Additional focus is given to traditional versus electronic creation, preservice and inservice uses, and reflections for teacher improvement and lifelong learning.

What's New in This Edition

Chapters include extended information on such topics as electronic portfolios and preparing for interviews. New "From the Real World" features preview chapter material and provide insight from current professionals. Along with these additions, there is more emphasis on applying Interstate New Teacher Assessment and Support Consortium (INTASC) standards and Teacher Work Sample (TWS) organization for the overall portfolio. Additional authentic examples (or artifacts) have been included to enhance the readers' understanding of the various concepts presented, as well as a glossary and an index for easier use.

How to Use This Book

Creating Your Teaching Portfolio is divided into two parts. Part One, "Understanding Portfolios," describes what a portfolio is, and discusses why it is important, what it should include, how to construct it, and how to organize it based on state, national, or content-area standards. Part Two, "Putting It All Together," has two main recurring themes. One theme is the need for reflection, and the other is the need for a practical portfolio. Part Two also discusses areas for which the portfolio can be used to illustrate and highlight proficiency. Additionally, we have provided an index for ease in locating specific subject areas, standards, or issues.

Acknowledgments

We wish to thank Cara Harvey-Labell, Allison McNamara, Emily Pecora, Margaret Leslie, and especially our patient editor, Chris Narozny, for their assistance in seeing this project through to its fruition. Also, our love and thanks to Joe, Jeff, and Noelle for putting up with us.

About the Authors

Patricia Rieman began her teaching career in 1982 in Tulsa, Oklahoma, with a bachelor's degree from the University of Tulsa. After teaching special education in the Tulsa public school system for 10½ years, Rieman moved to Illinois to complete her master's degree in the area of social and emotional disorders at Northern Illinois University. It was during this period that Rieman first began collaborating with Dr. Pamela Farris, and thus became involved in many projects for the Higher Education Division of McGraw-Hill.

After completing her masters, Rieman continued teaching high-incidence junior high school special education students in Loves Park, Illinois, and then worked with students with behavior disorders for four years in Sandwich, Illinois. In 1999, Rieman began her doctoral coursework in the Department of Literacy Education at Northern Illinois University. She has served as a clinical supervisor of students completing their second professional experiences in the Department of Teaching and Learning, and has taught a number of courses for the Department of Literacy Education. Rieman is currently an adjunct professor in the Department of Literacy Education and teaches undergraduate and graduate courses in reading methods, language arts, and children's literature. Her dissertation topic is an examination of influences on classroom reading instruction.

Rieman has created many student study guides, online resources, and instructor's manuals for McGraw-Hill, and helped create FolioLive. In addition to her work with McGraw-Hill, Rieman has also worked with Dr. Jerry Johns and Roberta Berglund on a content-area reading strategies text for Kendall/Hunt Publishing.

Jeanne Okrasinski taught for eight years as a Grades 5–11 teacher of math, social sciences, and language arts. She also served as the teacher representative to the Parent Teacher Organization (PTO) and as a volleyball and soccer coach. While completing her master's degree from Northern Illinois University in curriculum and instruction with a multicultural emphasis, Okrasinski taught English rhetoric and composition, tutored English as a Second Language (ESL) students, and also supervised undergraduate students in their final student teaching experiences. From 2001 to 2002, Okrasinski was the Northern Illinois University coordinator for alternative certification. Additionally, she served as an assistant in the preparation for the College of Education's National Council for Accreditation of Teacher Education (NCATE) review.

Okrasinski is currently an adjunct professor in the Department of Teaching and Learning, teaching undergraduate and graduate students in the areas of social sciences, middle school organization, and classroom management. She is completing her dissertation on the topic of curricular philosophy in middle school teaming.

This is Okrasinski's first experience working with McGraw-Hill, and her first publication.

PART I

Understanding Portfolios

1

Teaching Portfolios: What Are They and Why Do You Need Them?

When thinking about best practices, authentic assessment ranks very highly. A **portfolio** is an assessment tool that allows the creator to put his or her best foot forward and document the knowledge and skills mastered through the learning process. In the past, preservice teachers would simply take classes, complete clinical assignments, and pass the certification tests. This has changed dramatically now that most states have moved to standards-based programs. Such programs are built on "the idea that educators need to present evidence of their competence relative to standards that include[d] evidence of student accomplishments" (Ashford & Deering, 2003, p. 22). Portfolios have since been established as the customary method for displaying teaching competence and content-area knowledge.

❧ The Professional Portfolio as a Concept

Portfolios allow teachers the space to identify their learning through reflection and examination of artifacts. Reflection will help you determine the areas for which you may need further guidance and instruction in order to feel competent in your skills. On the other hand, as you review the artifacts in your portfolio, you will have a clear picture of all that you have accomplished during your preservice journey. The portfolio is an ongoing, holistic, and comprehensive overview of your development in the teaching profession. You will determine the evidence that you believe represents your best practice in the classroom and in the school as you create your goals for the future. One of those goals is probably to land your first teaching job. The time and effort that you give to the creation of your portfolio will communicate volumes about your work ethic, teaching philosophy, and personality. Remember that the portfolio can be created to project the image you want others to see.

Whether you are creating a portfolio for a graduation or class requirement, or simply for personal gain, it is important to know why you are creating this showcase of your skills. For every document and photo that eventually will become part of your portfolio, careful consideration must be given to the small details. The portfolio is an important tool, one that teacher education researcher Phyllis Learner describes as:

- Purposeful and selective
- Diverse and ongoing
- Reflective and collaborative (Sadker & Sadker, 2000)

We will use Learner's six characteristics to organize the next portion of this chapter. Learner's ideas describe the essential ingredients in creating a meaningful portfolio. Employing these characteristics will help you build a straightforward and effective portfolio.

Purposeful and Selective

Your teaching portfolio will show your intentional alertness to detail in the items you chose to include. Each section will have a specific purpose. Learner recommends basing your portfolio upon a set of national standards. Another possibility is to research the school districts you are applying to and make the portfolio specific to their priorities. For example, if they are currently advocating full inclusion in their classrooms, your portfolio will reflect your ability to team-teach, work with parents, utilize support staff effectively, and appropriately modify your curriculum and instruction.

As you complete your course credits, hours of study, and years of experience in college and in your preservice student teaching endeavors, you are accumulating an ongoing, vast array of outstanding examples of your growth as an educator. You will have papers of which you are particularly proud, glowing narrative descriptions of your first

From the Real World

The Need for Practicality and Courtesy

—Patricia Rieman

Just last week, a colleague shared with me a problem an administrator of a nearby school district had experienced. It seems this district has approximately 11 teaching positions to fill, and there are over 5,000 applicants. In addition to the overwhelming amount of paperwork to be sorted through, another frustration is the new practice of e-mailing video clips. By utilizing technology and no small amount of audacity, applicants are now circumventing secretaries, appointments, and even the U.S. Postal Service by e-mailing unsolicited video clips of themselves to the superintendents and principals in districts. Imagine how long it takes to download each of those e-mails—you cannot delete incoming mail on its way in. Then, whoever is waiting (and waiting) for those e-mails to download sees just what the waiting was for. Now envision how the recipient of those e-mails feels about the senders—would you want your name to be recognized in such a context?

This is just one example of the myriad possible misuses of portfolios and their components, and it is a perfect segue into a text about creating and using practical portfolios.

Initiative is important, as is demonstration of technological skills; however, equally important are courtesy, organization, and understanding of protocol and one's place in the natural order of interviewing. Within this text you will find descriptions, explanations, and examples of various styles of portfolios and artifacts.

time in front of a group of students, and critical but encouraging evaluations from your supervisors. Most important, a well-organized portfolio displays the desire and knowledge necessary to become a dedicated professional and a lifelong learner. You must be highly selective in choosing which documents you make part of your portfolio, ensuring that these selections fit with the overall purpose and theme you are trying to achieve.

Borko, Michalec, Timmons, and Siddle (1997) identified and discussed several purposes for creating portfolios. Which of these purposes is evident in your portfolio?

- For evaluation and to secure employment
- To be graded, such as in a professional seminar
- To represent your teaching philosophy and style
- To provide a stimulus for reflection on your teaching and to develop your identity
- To serve as a vehicle for advancing your professional development

Diverse and Ongoing

Remember that your professors and administrators are interested in more than a one-dimensional documentation of courses you have taken and clinicals you have experienced. Any experiences with children and the community will help demonstrate your abilities and dedication as a teacher. Keep your portfolio diverse by including items that display your involvement with university organizations, youth clubs, or community groups. Make the presentation engaging by using a variety of mediums: photos, news articles, letters of thanks, certificates of achievement, and other worthy entries.

Ongoing refers to the need to keep your portfolio current. Regardless of your level of experience as an educator, you will always be learning and growing. Your portfolio should display this growth. However, remember to be intentional: Use the artifacts that best represent your abilities, interests, and commitment without causing your portfolio to seem cluttered or inefficient.

Reflective and Collaborative

"In the infinite number of variables that influence America's schools and teachers, a standards-based teacher portfolio holds the potential for improving the professional competence of teachers and in turn student achievement" (Ashford & Deering, 2003, p. 23). As a reflective practitioner, you will constantly revisit and revise the contents of your portfolio. It is important to determine whether your portfolio conveys your intended message to its audience. **Reflection** is the ability to think about what you have done in the past so that you can apply it to the future. It requires revisiting and critically assessing lessons, discussions, and management issues, among other tasks, that you encounter every day. It also requires that you think about what strategies and teaching styles may best address the ideals of a lesson and fit the nature of the students in the classroom. Reflection is necessary for growth, and it is a good thing to practice every day. Keeping a journal of successes and failures will help you plan successful lessons in the future.

Collaborative is a term with several positive meanings. It might mean, for example, that you are a team player, willing to work with your colleagues, fellow staff members, parents, community, and students to provide the best possible education to your students. Collaborative also addresses the need to display the role others played in your portfolio. You may have team-taught a lesson in class or completed a group project. Perhaps you and your professor maintained a dialogue journal during your clinical experiences. A third possibility for collaboration involves asking others to provide feedback on your portfolio.

✄ Portfolio Benefits

Portfolios are useful tools for displaying your abilities to master certain knowledge, skills, and dispositions. These attributes are reflected in most national organization standards as well as specialized subject-area standards of professional growth and development. Each national organization will spell out these characteristics in slightly different terms; however, they all focus on the three main areas of knowledge, skills, and dispositions. Below we have given an example of a widely accepted national organization's standards, known as INTASC. Later we will discuss specific subject-matter standards in context.

Demonstrates Mastery of INTASC Standards

Teaching Standard

The **Interstate New Teacher Assessment and Support Consortium (INTASC)** is a "consortium of state education agencies and national educational organizations dedicated to the reform of the preparation, licensing, and ongoing professional development of teachers" (Council of Chief State School Officers, 2005). INTASC has identified 10 standards for what beginning teachers should know. Briefly, these components include:

1. Knowledge of subject
2. Learning and human development
3. Adapting instruction
4. Strategies
5. Motivation and classroom management
6. Communication skills
7. Planning
8. Assessment
9. Commitment
10. Partnerships (INTASC, 2004; Martin, 1999)

A majority of states have adopted INTASC as their licensing standards. Many states have reciprocal agreements for teacher certification; that is, they agree to accept one another's licensure programs. Accordingly, universities have made a concerted effort to move "from a traditional preparation system of state-prescribed courses and hours to one that was based on performance standards and required accompanying performance-based assessments" (Quatroche, Duarte, Huffman-Joley, & Watkins, 2002, p. 268). One may surmise that states adopt INTASC as a way to ensure that teachers across the nation are held to the same standards of accountability.

Demonstrates Mastery of Teacher Work Sample (TWS) Standards

Teaching
Standard

Those of you completing TWS evaluations will find a portfolio complements this approach by focusing your attention to each standard in clearly outlined sections. Following the TWS standards outlined by the Renaissance project or other associations, your portfolio will evidence the growth and learning that has occurred during your preprofessional experience. Teacher Work Samples are defined and discussed in-depth in Chapter 4.

Demonstrates Mastery of Subject-Specific Standards

If you are seeking certification as middle or secondary school teachers, or if you teach special classes such as music, art, and physical education, you will most likely utilize other sets of standards for your portfolio organization. For example, someone who wishes to teach eighth-grade social studies may use either the standards of the National Middle School Association or the National Council of Social Studies as ways of organizing artifacts. If you are unsure of your national organization, check the Appendix in the back of this book for a fairly comprehensive listing.

⚔ Examples of Portfolio Use

The portfolio you create will need to be adaptive and potentially last throughout your teaching career. During both your preservice and inservice years, the portfolio will prove an essential evaluation tool. It will assist your school leaders in identifying your current strengths and it will provide them with ideas for how you might improve in the classroom. In this section, we will explore different ways to use your portfolio both as a preservice teacher and as a teacher in the field.

Preservice Use

Preservice refers to teacher candidates who are undergoing coursework and clinical experiences to become certified, licensed educators. Throughout this text we will discuss a variety of ways to use your teaching portfolio. One early preservice use is to demonstrate your knowledge to your cooperating teachers so that they will have a better understanding of your current capabilities. This will lead to a clinical experience that can be tailored more specifically to areas in which you need further growth opportunities.

Another instance of preservice use occurs when you begin your job search. Districts seeking new teachers to join their staffs are in precarious positions. They must rely on subjective evaluations such as interviews, letters of recommendation from people who are strangers to them, and the word—possibly lip service—of those being interviewed. When employers read your portfolio, they have the opportunity to observe you through the pictures, lesson plans, and reflections that illustrate who you are. In Chapter 8 you will find further information on using your portfolio during interviews.

Inservice Use: Maintaining a Career Portfolio

Inservice refers to a certified, licensed educator. An ongoing **career portfolio** serves to keep records of those wonderful projects, bulletin boards, learning centers, and thematic units you have created as an inservice teacher. As the years fly by, the memories of those unique creations will fade and you will find yourself wishing you had kept copies of them to adapt for future students. You may be an experienced educator who wishes to teach in a different area, or you may be taking postgraduate classes and want to refer to all those wonderful activities you implemented when you student taught.

Finally, teaching portfolios provide times for reflection. Arends, Winitzky, and Tannenbaum (2001) define reflection as the ability and disposition to think deeply and make decisions about which strategy is appropriate at any given time. We educators often get so swept up in the day-to-day (or minute-to-minute) hectic world of teaching that we forget to stop and think about how our lessons have turned out, or how we feel about the day's events. Maintaining a portfolio gives you the opportunity to develop the healthy habit of reflecting on the success (or lack thereof) of a lesson. Whether or not you are using the TWS, saving student work provides evidence of your successful and not-so-successful lessons. It can provide validation for what you are doing when a lesson goes well. On the other hand, saving student work that shows how the lesson failed miserably provides valuable input as well. You can learn from your mistakes and chuckle ruefully as you come across the unfortunate samples years later. Either way, you are taking the time to consider the effects of your efforts—isn't that what we always want our students to do?

National Board for Professional Teaching Standards (NBPTS)

After you have taught for at least three years, you may wish to seek national certification. The **National Board for Professional Teaching Standards (NBPTS)** utilizes portfolios as the means to assess your competence and credentials. Created by the Carnegie Forum in the 1990s to recognize outstanding educators, the NBPTS identifies five core propositions and breaks them down into standards and goals for each individual discipline. The five propositions are:

1. Teachers are committed to students and their learning.
2. Teachers know the subjects they teach and how to teach those subjects to students.
3. Teachers are responsible for managing and monitoring student learning.
4. Teachers think systematically about their practice and learn from experience.
5. Teachers are members of learning communities. (NBPTS, 1999)

References

Arends, R. I., Winitzky, N. E., & Tannenbaum, M. D. (2001). *Exploring teaching.* Boston: McGraw-Hill.

Ashford, A., & Deering, P. (2003). *Middle level teacher preparation: The impact of the portfolio experience on teachers' professional development.* Paper presented at the annual meeting of the American Educational Research Association, Chicago.

Borko, H., Michalec, P., Timmons, M., & Siddle, J. (1997). Student teaching portfolios: A tool for promoting reflective practice. *Journal of Teacher Education, 48*(5), 345–357.

Council of Chief State School Officers. (2005). Retrieved from

http://www.ccsso.org/projects/Interstate_New_Teacher_Assessment_and_Support_Consortium/

Farris, P. J. (1999). *Teaching, bearing the torch,* 2nd ed. Boston: McGraw-Hill.

The Interstate New Teacher Assessment and Support Consortium. (2004). Retrieved from

http://www.ccsso.org/projects/Interstate_New_Teacher_Assessment_and_Support_Consortium/

Martin, D. B. (1999). *The portfolio planner: Making professional portfolios work for you.* Upper Saddle River, NJ: Merrill.

The National Board for Professional Teaching Standards. (2004). Retrieved from

http://www.nbpts.org/about/index.c3fm

Quatroche, D., Duarte, V., Huffman-Joley, G., & Watkins, S. (2002). Redefining assessment of preservice teachers: Standards based exit portfolios. *The Teacher Educator, 37* (4), 268–281.

The Renaissance Partnership for Improving Teacher Quality Project.

http://fp.uni.edu/itq

Sadker, M., & Sadker, D. (2000). *Teachers, schools, & society,* 5th ed. Boston: McGraw-Hill.

Suggested Resources

Print

Constantino, P. M., & De Lorenzo, M. N. (2006). *Developing a professional teaching portfolio: A guide for success.* College Park: University of Maryland.

Web Sites

This site from the University of Texas at El Paso is "part of an ongoing dialogue at the University of Texas at El Paso on the nature of teaching as scholarly work, its development in professional terms and its review." Go to:

http://cetal.utep.edu/resources/portfolios/

Washington State University provides this site that includes a general format, outline of a teaching portfolio, examples of teaching portfolios, and references. Go to:

http://www.wsu.edu/provost/teaching.htm

Compiling Your Portfolio

Your portfolio is not only a manifestation of who you are, but it is also a visualization of your educational philosophy. In Chapter 1, we briefly discussed your purpose in creating a portfolio. Whether you are assigned to create a portfolio or you are constructing one by choice, the artifacts and design that you use will reflect your teaching style and philosophy of education. For example, your choice to include graphic displays of your interactions with small groups of students instead of pictures of you standing at the front of the class will speak to your preference for maintaining a student-centered classroom. If you have not solidified your philosophy of education, we encourage you to do so now as it will be easier to complete the portfolio with a philosophical foundation already in place.

✛ Recognizing and Expressing Your Philosophy

Teachers represent the collective wisdom of our culture and insist on maintaining the integrity of the methods, substance and structures of disciplinary knowledge. In the face of pressures to portray knowledge in weak and diluted forms, they remain firm. Their role, however, is not just to reinforce the status quo. Rather, appreciative of the fact that there are multiple perspectives and interpretations in each discipline, accomplished teachers encourage students to question prevailing canons and assumptions to help them think for themselves.

The National Board for Professional Teaching Standards, 2004

This quotation eloquently states the NBPTS's definition of the role of teachers. The definition is comprehensive and thus difficult to argue. Your philosophy of teaching will be one of the multiple perspectives to which it refers. When considering the subject(s) you will teach, your philosophy will be reflected in your actions within the classroom and curriculum. Professional decisions that you make are driven by your beliefs in the following areas:

- Why should your subject be taught?
- What are the desired outcomes for your students following your lesson?
- How will the knowledge that students gain impact society?
- How will you present the lesson?
- What is the best way for your students to learn?
- When are students developmentally ready to learn your subject?
- How will you assess students' mastery of the subject?
- What is your style of classroom management?
- To what extent will parents be involved in your lessons?
- Will you assign homework? If so, for what purpose?

As you can imagine, the possible philosophical questions are innumerable. These 10 questions are but the tip of the iceberg of educational philosophies. In this chapter, we will explore some of the better-known philosophies of teaching with the goal of guiding you to recognize the theory behind some of your own philosophies.

✛ Basic Educational Philosophies

In your foundation of education courses, you will receive more extensive instruction on the intricacies and history of various educational philosophies. We will provide a brief overview of the most well-known educational philosophies as a basis for constructing your portfolio.

Idealism

Idealism, the oldest known philosophy, is associated with Plato, Descartes, Kant, and Spinoza, among others. Idealists tend to believe that all students are capable of being positive, contributing

From the Real World

A Spanish Teacher's Philosophy of Education
Patience Henkle

My philosophical beliefs about teaching, learning, human development and leadership have all been shaped by reading and studying the ideas of John Dewey. As a student of education, I have been aware of John Dewey's ideas for many years. When I taught Spanish at the high school level, I tried to create a curriculum that was in line with Dewey's theories. Because Dewey has insisted that students resent atmospheres that are more autocratic than democratic in nature, I tried to fill the role of facilitator rather than dictator. Students were always active; we sang, danced, talked, played games, ate authentic foods and went on field trips. Also, Spanish lends itself well to cooperative learning. Students often worked in cooperative groups creating dialogues, skits or writing in Spanish.

One very poignant and meaningful passage from Dewey's *Experience and Education* discusses the importance of the present moment. Each instant should be valued in and of itself rather than as preparation for some greater future moment. Dewey explains,

> The ideal of using the present simply to get ready for the future contradicts itself. It omits, and even shuts out, the very conditions by which a person can be prepared for his future. We always live at the time we live and not at some other time, and only by extracting at each present time the full meaning of each present experience are we prepared for doing the same thing in the future. This is the only preparation, which in the long run amounts to anything.

Learning for the sake of learning should be emphasized at an early age. This is what will create life-long learners.

members of society, and that discipline matters can be handled "in-house" by simply talking rationally with the disruptive student. Idealistic teachers believe that students should find joy in education because they seek the truth, and that the curriculum should be based on cultural heritage (Farris, 1999). Read the descriptors and decide if you agree with this philosophy.

- My students will want to learn the worthwhile knowledge that I have to offer them because they are rational individuals.
- I will teach my students critical knowledge of the past and help them to master facts and universal truths.
- By thinking rationally, students will not only learn the subjects that I teach, but will also understand our society's traditional values.
- The curriculum I teach is based on time-tested information and good literature.

Perennialism and Essentialism

If you see your role in education as that of a moral, intellectual authority figure, you may find your beliefs lie within the philosophy of **perennialism.** Perennialist programs often use classical literature, and their curricula require students to undergo challenging, rigorous courses.

Teachers who believe that the primary purpose of their curriculum is to transmit useful skills by focusing on academics are considered to be followers of **essentialism.** Essentialists believe that the role of schools is to create successful citizens (Arends, 2001). Students taught by essentialists can expect to be tested often for mastery, and to experience "skill and drill" lessons (Farris, 1999). Here are four descriptors for this philosophical area. Do your thoughts coincide with these ideas?

- Education should promote intellectual growth and help students become competent members of society.
- What we teach should concentrate on the core content areas—math, science, English, and social studies. This information does not change over time.
- As teachers, we should expect students to master the concepts and principles we teach in the core content areas.
- Teachers are the authority in the classroom and must have expertise in the subject areas that they teach.

Progressivism, Experimentalism, and Pragmatism

Progressivists believe that students must be prepared to live in an ever-changing society. Cooperative learning, hands-on activities, intrinsic rewards, and the role of teacher as facilitator rather than expert are all basic tenets of **progressivism. Experimentalist** educators focus on child-centered activities, and allow much time for play because children need to play in order to learn to compete and to cooperate (Farris, 1999). These educators believe that all subject matter should be connected both to other subjects and to the students' home lives. **Pragmatists** tend to be problem solvers who value use of the scientific method. They may use quality literature to teach both language arts and social studies in integrated units. Students of pragmatists will be encouraged to apply their knowledge in authentic, hands-on experiences. Read these few statements regarding progressivism, experimentalism, and pragmatism, and judge how strongly you concur with them.

- I want to promote democracy as a way of life and help my students become creative self-learners.
- Learning is a process that accompanies living. The learning process should then be active and relevant to students' daily lives.
- As a teacher, I want to guide my students in their learning so that they can solve problems on their own. The rules of scientific inquiry are a handy tool that all students should learn.
- What I teach the students should center on their individual interests and promote interdisciplinary instruction.

Existentialism

Do you find yourself considering all angles of a problem? Do you believe that the implications of your decision will be far-reaching? Do you often rebel against traditional approaches to teaching? If you, like your predecessors Jean-Paul Sartre and Friedrich Nietzsche, believe that you must always be free to choose and take responsibility for your choices, you are affiliated with the existentialist philosophy. **Existentialism** is difficult to define because to define it would be to confine it (eliminating your freedom)—which would make it no longer existentialist. Existentialist educators focus on empowering their students with individual freedom, and stress arts and literature over math and science (Farris, 1999). If you would like to put your existential self in a box, determine if the following ideas fit your teaching philosophy.

- I want my students to be active citizens who voice their opinions and participate in civic functions.
- In my teaching, I want to put equality, liberty, and human life at the center of discussions, including those of democracy and citizenship.
- As a teacher, I am a critical intellectual. I want my students to question how knowledge is produced, distributed, and accepted.
- Through my teaching, students will become dedicated to self and social empowerment, will understand the implications of their actions, and will be able to discuss social issues with knowledge and understanding.

Social Reconstructionism

Finally, there is **social reconstructionism,** sometimes referred to simply as *reconstructionism.* Reconstructionists believe that the function of schools is to teach students to examine social problems and, ultimately, to change society for the better. The theory that schools should model the ideal world is a good example of reconstructionism (Arends, 2001). Read the descriptors for this philosophy and see if you agree with this theory.

- Education is meant to change people and the world. It will improve society and reform it for a new generation.
- As a teacher, the skills and information that you help students acquire will be used to identify and solve problems in society. The students will be actively concerned with what is happening in today's world.
- I will help students see what challenges our world is facing and help them develop a passion for resolving the problems confronting humankind.
- The material that I teach students should focus on social, economic, and political problems.

✥ Compiling Your Portfolio

Deciding which artifacts to include in your portfolio is always difficult because you have a wealth of good ideas, documents, and pictures from which to choose. Selecting artifacts that speak to your philosophy of education sends a clear message to the school interview team as to what they can expect from you both in and out of the classroom. (See Artifact 2.1 for an example.) Another idea is to choose artifacts that reflect the mission or goals of the school district in which you work or to which you are applying for a job. This may mean that your portfolio is flexible and includes different artifacts suited to the diverse occasions for its use. Depending upon your time constraints and organizational skills, this may or may not be a viable option for you. The following outline provides a general guide to the categories and items suggested for inclusion in a teaching portfolio. It is important to bear in mind that your portfolio must reflect your personality more than your ability to follow a how-to portfolio "recipe."

2.1   Artifact

The following philosophy of education reflects elementary education major Lisa Owens's priorities and values.

Philosophy of Education

As an educator, one of the most important things to do is meet the individual needs of the students in the classroom. All children can learn with the right type of instruction and differentiation. Each student learns in a different way so teachers need to be able to adapt their instruction to each child. Teachers need to know how their students learn in order to provide them with appropriate opportunities. Students must be challenged in the classroom, yet the goals set for them should still be obtainable. It is crucial to make each child in the classroom feel as confident and competent as possible. Each student should leave every day feeling some measure of success. While meeting individual needs, it is also important to meet the needs of the whole class. A classroom should promote a positive environment that is conductive to learning. Student needs to feel included, accepted, and respected in a classroom in order to feel confident to continue the learning process.

Another important element of education is that learning should be student-centered not teacher-centered. If students are given a chance to self-direct their learning, they will have a better understanding of it and will enjoy what they are learning more. Students should have a voice and be allowed to give input to the teacher on the structure of the classroom environment. This nurtures good decision-making skills and critical thinking skills. Education is a combination of learning experiences and content. Engaged learning is effective learning. This can be achieved by promoting hands-on activities, student-led discussions, and cooperative learning groups. When engaging learning occurs, a student feels empowered to succeed in life. Above all, learning needs to be made meaningful.

A final element of education is the parent–teacher relationship. This relationship can improve the child's education and performance in the classroom. Through communication with parents, teachers are able to discover so many more details about their students which they can apply in the classroom to help them succeed. Weekly notes home, phone calls involving positive and negative experiences, and conferences can help achieve this. Everyone benefits from this relationship because it can make the child's educational experience more meaningful and more successful, which is every teacher's ultimate goal.

TWS: The Teacher Work Sample (TWS) model provides a structured format for selecting artifacts. Artifacts should be examples of your work and student products from a designated unit of study that you implemented during your clinical experience. When determining which artifacts to use, you should follow the same guidelines as described for INTASC-driven and all other portfolios.

Teaching
Standard

✄ Providing Rationales for Artifacts

A prime time to reflect upon your previous experiences and philosophy of education is when you are choosing artifacts for your professional portfolio (see Artifact 2.2). As you select the artifacts that best represent your teaching abilities and values, consider the following questions:

- Why does this particular artifact appeal to you?
- What should your university evaluators or future employers learn about you from this artifact?
- What qualities does this artifact reveal about you?
- What INTASC category would this artifact fall into?

2.2   Artifact

Review Melissa Denna's artifact rationale. Does this rationale reflect the selection criteria?

Artifact for Standard Seven: Instructional Planning Skills

Name of Artifact: Visual Study Guide
Date: November 7, 2001
Rationale:

During my second professional semester many of my fifth-grade students came to me concerned about their social studies test grades. They were having a hard time remembering the required content on the tests. I was thrilled that they came to me, but I was confused about how to help. Before I could help I needed to find out what content they were responsible for, what the curricular goals were, and most importantly what method to use so they could remember what they needed to know.

With all of this in mind, I searched through their social studies book and found the upcoming test. According to Bloom's Taxonomy, the objectives for the unit were mostly comprehension and application level. I took this into account and created a visual study guide for part of the content. First, I drew this very simple picture that related to what they were responsible for knowing. Then, I had my students view this illustration on an overhead transparency for sixty seconds. I then asked the students to explain what they remembered seeing. Throughout their discussion I listed their ideas and guided their answers by changing their vocabulary to that listed in the drawing. Together we created a caption: "The missionaries came from South America to North America and taught Native Americans their religion, which was Christianity." This visualization method raised about 80% of my students' test scores on the next social studies test. This method was exactly the approach they needed to remember the vital information.

- Do you already have enough artifacts included in your portfolio that cover the same standards or category as the item you are currently reviewing? If so, leave it out!
- What will you say about this artifact when discussing it with whomever is evaluating you?

Artifact rationales are the brief descriptions you write to explain your choice of artifacts for inclusion in your portfolio.

� Organizing A Teaching Portfolio

Gather your artifact options together. One organizational strategy that works well is to create a box system for storage based upon the INTASC or other standards. Write the number of the standard and its description on the outside of the box so that you can easily distribute the artifacts into the correct boxes. It is time to sort through your options and choose those that best reflect your personality, philosophy, and skills. The following suggested table of contents may also be used to create an organizational system for artifacts in a non-INTASC portfolio.

Suggested Table of Contents for a Teaching Portfolio (*Artifacts 2.3–2.7,*
showing examples of various elements of this suggested table of contents, follow.)

A. Statement of Teaching Philosophy
B. Credentials
    1. Letters of reference
    2. Résumé (*see Artifact 2.4*)
    3. Official transcript
    4. Record of courses
    5. Teaching certificate
    6. Endorsements
C. Teaching-Related Experiences
    1. Preprofessional clinical experiences (*see Artifact 2.5*)
    2. Employment in child-related fields
    3. Volunteer work with children
    4. Student teaching experiences, TWS or INTASC standards
        a. sample lesson plans
        b. reflective journal
        c. sample student work
        d. photos of bulletin boards or projects you created
        e. letters from students or parents
        f. evaluations by university supervisor
        g. evaluations by cooperating/mentor teacher
    5. Classroom management plan (*see Artifact 2.6*)
        a. sample discipline referral form
        b. sample letters to parents
        c. sample team policy
    6. Curricular modifications
    7. How your lesson plans reflect state or national goals (*see Artifact 2.7*)
D. Community Involvement
    1. Descriptions of volunteerism (other than earlier mentioned child-related activities)
    2. Copies of articles concerning or actual certificates of local awards or scholarships won
    3. Photos or articles concerning community, religious, or civic group participation
E. Professional Memberships and Honor Societies
    1. Certificates of membership in student chapters of professional groups, such as Council for Exceptional Children, International Reading Association, National Council for Teachers of Mathematics, National Education Association, etc.
    2. Certificates of membership or articles concerning membership in academic or service-related honor societies such as Phi Delta Kappa, Mortar Board, Omicron Delta Kappa, etc.
F. Extracurricular Activities
    1. Experience with sports you would be able to coach
    2. Experiences with journalism, yearbook, or other media
    3. Experiences with other club activities, such as chess, international clubs, or career-related clubs
    4. Roles of leadership in the above organizations

2.3   Artifact

Below you will view Carla Raynor's table of contents for her teaching portfolio. In Chapter 8 you will be able to view the brochure that Carla organized according to these contents.

Table of Contents
I. Content Knowledge
    A. Teaching Social Studies
    B. Adapting Dental Unit
II. Human Development & Learning
    A Enhancing Language Arts & Writing
    B. Developing New Skills
III. Diversity
    A. Integrating Multiple Disciplines
    B. Meeting Individual Needs
IV. Planning for Instruction
    A. Writing Organized Lesson Plans
    B. Providing Detailed Instruction
V. Learning Environment
    A Reading & Listening Activity
    B. Enhancing Basal Lesson

VI. Instructional Delivery
    A. Designing Cooperative Learning Lesson
    B. Interdisciplinary Lesson
VII. Communication
    A. Increasing Language Arts Capabilities
    B. Using Variety of Communication
VIII. Assessment
    A. Designing Unit Assessments
    B. Creating Informal Assessments
IX. Collaborative Relationships
    A. Communicating with Parents
    B. Communicating with Students
X. Reflection & Professional Growth
    A. Practicing Self-Reflection
    B. Participating in Conferences & Class
XI. Professional Conduct
    A. Professional Training
    B. Faculty Training

2.4   Artifact

Susan LeMay's résumé is posted on her Web site. Notice how Susan manages to keep such a large amount of information well-organized and succinct.

Susan LeMay
4617 Oak Terrace
Stevenson, IL 55127

Objective
To obtain a teaching position at the elementary level.

Education
Northern Illinois University, DeKalb, IL
Bachelor of science in education, December 2002
Major: Elementary education
Certification: IL Type 03

McHenry County College, Crystal Lake, IL
Associate of Science, December 2002.

Additional Qualifications
College classes and experience working with students with special needs and IEPs
Excellent computer skills: Edline, Grade Quick, Excel, Word, Outlook, PowerPoint, Publisher, and Web design.

Teaching Experience
Substitute Elementary Teacher (August 2004 to Present): Cary District 26, Prairie Grove District 46, Crystal Lake District 47, Huntley District 158, Marengo District 165

Continued

2.4 Artifact *Continued*

7th-Grade Science Teacher (2003–2004): Cary Junior High, Cary, IL

- Presented hands-on, inquiry-based lessons on the scientific method, evolution, life science, matter, physics, human biology, ecology, and earth science.
- Worked closely with the resource teacher, differentiating lessons as needed for students with learning disabilities and autism.
- Member of the after-school homework committee; helped students understand and complete assignments from other classes, and encouraged independent study skills. Volunteered during track meets, school dances, and the seventh-grade trip to St. Louis.

Student Teaching—4th Grade (Fall 2002; 12 weeks): May Whitney Elementary, Lake Zurich, IL

- Compiled and taught a thematic unit based on the Northeast region.
- Created a 10-day-long ecology unit for the 4th-grade teaching team to keep.

Junior Clinical Experience—Middle School (Spring 2002): Rockford Environmental Science Academy, Rockford, IL

- Compiled science units and taught 6th-grade ecosystem class using hands-on labs.
- Accompanied students on field trips, including a water study project at Rock Cut State Park in Rockford and several museums in Chicago.

Sophomore Clinical Experience—5th Grade (Fall 2001): McCleary Elementary School, Aurora, IL

- Created and implemented social studies and writing units for 5th-grade students.

Related Experience

Pre-kindergarten and Summer Program Teacher (1995–2003): Barlina House Preschool, Crystal Lake, IL (Pre-K and 4-to-5-year old classes)

- Created and implemented thematic units, reading incentive programs, journal activities, daily math and science activities, monthly newsletters, and progress reports.
- Attended and presented workshops, coordinated field trips, recruited parent volunteers, and arranged evening family programs.

Preschool Teacher and Substitute Teacher (2001–2003): St. Paul's Preschool, Crystal Lake, IL

Classroom Volunteer (Spring 2002): Littlejohn Elementary School, DeKalb, IL (Bilingual, multiage classroom K–2)

- Assisted Spanish-speaking children in English with language arts, math, and science lessons.

Adult Education Volunteer (2000–2001): McHenry County College, Crystal Lake, IL

- Volunteered in both Adult Literacy and English as a Second Language programs.
- Created learning games to help develop English proficiency for Spanish-speaking adults.
- Followed a basal reading program to help develop reading proficiency for adults with brain injuries and mental retardation.

Director/Teacher of Crystal Lake Park District Summer Camp (Summer 1996): Crystal Lake, IL

- Directed a six-person staff and 80 students within a structured, nature-oriented day camp program for children ages 3–6.

Preschool Teacher (1990–1995): Friendship House Daycare, Crystal Lake, IL

Professional Organizations

- National Council for Exceptional Children
- National Science Teacher's Association
- National Council for the Social Studies
- National Education Association
- Kappa Delta Pi

Interests

Bicycle tours, camping, hiking, kayaking, painting, running, yoga, swimming, visiting museums, travel, reading, and teaching.

2.5   Artifact

The following artifact from elementary education major Sherri Johnson demonstrates the diversity Johnson has experienced in her first and second professional clinical experiences.

Taylor Elementary vs. Rickman Science Academy Reflection on Clinical Experiences

Clinical experiences during the teacher education program at Southern College have offered me many different perspectives as a preservice teacher. The school's professional education program consists of four semesters in which preservice teachers complete two clinicals and a student teaching semester, concluding with a final semester of additional classes designed for reflecting on the experience. Having a variety of clinical experiences can help teachers gain insights into different classroom environments and gain an understanding the needs of the students of today. I have been lucky to have the opportunity to experience my preservice clinicals at two very different schools, Taylor Elementary School and Rickman Science Academy (RSA) Middle School. Comparing these two schools has helped me understand diversity among young learners and prepare ways in which I may become a better educator.

My first classroom experience was with a fourth-grade class at Taylor Elementary School in Taylor, Illinois. Taylor is a small town, located about 5 miles from the college. The Taylor Elementary report card indicates the school's district had the following demographics in 2003: 73% Caucasian, 10% African American,

14% Hispanic, 3% Asian, and 0.3% Native American. 31% of students in the district were from low-income families.

The semester of my clinical happened to correspond with the school's grand opening in the fall of 2004. Preservice teachers at Taylor Elementary had the opportunity to watch the school grow as a fresh institution, and observe the unification of new students and faculty. My college classes that semester were unique because classes were also held at Taylor Elementary. For six weeks, preservice teachers would have a couple of hours in the morning at the clinical classroom during language arts, then go down the hall to a reserved classroom for our college classes.

Since it was a "charter school," many of the planned resources were not yet in place. For example, many of the computers with Internet access were yet to be installed and fully operational. However, within the first few weeks of operation, I observed many uses of the available technology. Within that first semester, students were using laptops to complete assignments and camcorders to film various projects. Each classroom was equipped with computers with access to the Internet.

My observations were mostly in the fourth-grade classroom during language arts and math. It was an interesting experience to learn about the students' needs. Educationally, their needs are focused on getting into the flow of being in school, gaining knowledge of beneficial strategies for learning, and learning routines. The goals of classroom activities were to get the students engaged in their learning, teach students strategies for learning, encourage group work, and

Displaying Credentials

If you are writing a résumé and have not yet obtained a degree or teacher certification, you can state your anticipated date of graduation and the certificates for which you will be applying and testing. Also stress the importance of other areas of employment that involved working with children or roles of leadership.

Confidentiality Issues

As you work with students, you will get to know them and want to discuss their joys and failures, frustrations, and "a-ha" moments. It is your responsibility to ensure the anonymity of your students whether you are discussing a written reflection during class, attending a get-together with other student teachers, or creating a document for your portfolio. A simple solution for disguising the identity of your students is to change names, leave out promote self-efficacy. Difficulties in the classroom usually consisted of keeping students in order and on task. My responsibilities in the classroom were to mainly observe, to teach a couple of lessons, and to assist students with needs. Being in the same environment as our students was a great advantage for us because we could actually see and interact with a "real life" school setting which helped in applying concepts and theories learned in our methods classes, as well as developing our relationship with our cooperating teachers and other faculty members.

My second professional semester in spring 2005 included observations of students at RSA middle school, located on the west side of Steuben, Illinois. RSA is a relatively newer middle school for sixth to eighth grade, about five years old. Diversity among the demographics of the students was great. RSA's report card indicated that the student population in 2004 held 1,225 students. Demographics included the following: 40% Caucasian, 43% African American, 16% Hispanic, 2% Asian, 0.2% Native American. 58% of students in the district were from low-income families. Even though the demographics at RSA greatly differ from those of Taylor Elementary, the learning and developmental needs of students at both schools are unique to the ages of the students.

During my clinical observations, I observed a seventh-grade environmental science classroom. I took my clinical experience at RSA as a "mini student teaching experience." I was responsible for helping my teacher create a unit plan and teaching for the three weeks I was there. I learned a lot teaching the students at RSA. The goals of classroom activities focused on students' learning and the science curriculum. The educational needs of adolescent students are focused on their development stages. The most important lesson I learned was teaching the students life lessons and respect. Difficulties in the classroom included teaching students to be respectful, the importance of education in regard to their futures, and adapting the curriculum to meet the needs of students at different learning levels.

In conclusion, the diversity among schools today is a challenge in our classrooms. To become better educators, we need to learn each of our students' needs and center our teaching to meet the needs of students in our classrooms. One way that Taylor and RSA were similar was the positive energy from the faculty at both schools. Most of the staff members seemed to be welcoming and helpful to myself as well as the students. They kept a positive attitude toward students' learning and behavior management. Some ways I noticed how the schools differed was through my experiences in the classrooms. There was a very large difference in the education needs of the students between fourth grade and seventh grade. At the elementary level, students' needs are based on routine and understanding fundamental ideas of learning. On the other hand, in middle school, the focus is on guiding students on the right path by encouraging the students to become involved, by teaching the students material that engages their interests, and by facilitating appropriate behaviors. I have learned that my greatest challenges as a teacher are to understand the needs of my students, motivate my students, present challenging lessons for all levels of learning, and provide an optimal learning environment.

information regarding school and class, and avoid dates if possible. You will also benefit from contacts with parents. If you include any information in your portfolio regarding contact with parents about certain students, you will need to take precautions to protect both parent and student confidentiality. Further information on this topic may be found in Chapter 5. Additionally, the Appendices include a reproducible form for your use in obtaining consent to use a student's work or photograph in your portfolio.

✄ Considerations

First impressions are permanent and can make or break your opportunity with a district. It is important to research the school districts you are interested in before you organize your portfolio for interviews. Regardless of the type of district you choose to apply to, appropriate documents include a table of

2.6   Artifact

Michael Kosky is pursuing a major in school counseling. His management plan includes understanding the important role his personality plays in counselor–student relationships.

As a counselor in a school, I believe these three qualities are needed in order for my students to feel accepted and willing to come to me:

1. Empathy: I strive to put myself in a student's shoes, whether it is a student seeking help with semester course planning or a personal issue or crisis. By seeking to truly understand a student's needs or why a student needs help, I feel I can support the student while also possibly providing him or her with alternative information or solutions.
2. Congruency: When students get to know me as genuine, consistent, and thoughtful, and know that I am always willing to listen to them, then they are more likely to enter into an effective counseling relationship. Once an effective counseling relationship is established with students, then career and college planning, academic planning, and crisis management become more meaningful and successful.
3. Consistency: It is very important that the students know what to expect when they come see me. They need to know that I will not say one thing today, and something different the next day. If they know I will be supporting them through both the easy and tough times, and if I treat them the same way, they will know I am someone who can help them in a time of need.

2.7   Artifact

Eric Spooner teaches elementary special education students in Tulsa, Oklahoma. Eric uses this checklist to manage his portfolio artifacts, as well as to align them with Oklahoma Learning Standards.

OAAP Checklist of Best Work Pieces of Evidence

Student's Name—Third Grade

Description	Collected?	Documented?	Notes
Extended Academic Standards Domains			
Reading (Language Arts)—5 pieces			
1			
2			
3			
4			
5			
Writing (Language Arts)—5 pieces			
1			
2			
3			
4			
5			

Mathematics—5 pieces

1 _____

2 _____

3 _____

4 _____

5 _____

Science—5 pieces

1 _____

2 _____

3 _____

4 _____

5 _____

Content Standards Domains

Personal & Home Management—videotape

1 _____

Community Living—2 pieces

1 _____

2 _____

Job & Work Opportunities—2 pieces

1 _____

2 _____

Recreation & Leisure—2 pieces

1 _____

2 _____

contents to make your portfolio simple to use, a record of courses to display the courses you have completed successfully, and a résumé focusing on your experiences with children in and out of the classroom.

References

Arends, R. I., Winitzky, N. E., & Tannenbaum, M. D. (2001). *Exploring teaching*. Boston: McGraw-Hill.

Farris, P. J. (1999). *Teaching, bearing the torch*, 2nd ed. Boston: McGraw-Hill.

The National Board for Professional Teaching Standards. (2004). Retrieved March 8, 2005, from http://www.nbpts.org/about/index.cfm

Suggested Resources

Web Sites

For more information on writing résumés and other employment tips, go to:

http://www.virtualresume.com/

Another engaging site is the "Damn Good Résumé" Web site. For suggested readings, examples of résumés, Web links, and other relevant information, go to:

http://www.damngood.com/

For examples of résumés, writing tips, and related links, go to:

http://www.4resumes.com/

For information on *Teaching Philosophy*, a journal for philosophy teachers at all levels, with Michael Goldman, Editor, go to:

http://www.pdcnet.org/teachph.html

Online Resources in Teaching Philosophy Web page:

http://www.erraticimpact.com/html/philosophy_pedagogy.htm

Frequently Asked Questions about the Philosophy of Teaching Statement Web page:

http://www.oic.id.ucsb.edu/TA/port-FAQ.html

CHAPTER 3

Selecting Your Portfolio Style

What style of portfolio best calls attention to your strengths? Your personality? In addition to your appearance, attitude, and responses to questions, your portfolio is an extremely important portrayal of your skills, knowledge, and values. There are many style options to consider when designing your portfolio. From the type of stationery and font used to the artifacts you choose to include, there are myriad decisions to be made.

In this chapter, we will discuss the *traditional* three-ring-binder portfolio and expand into descriptions of *electronic* portfolios, both *digital* and *Web based*. We will highlight the positive and negative attributes of each and provide links to Web sites for further information, and templates and samples available to download. Once you have established your philosophical foundation for the portfolio and have begun exploring the variety of artifacts to include, it is time to choose the format that will present your professional best.

Portfolio Qualities

When designing your portfolio, you should consider both aesthetic and efferent qualities. **Aesthetics** relate to the emotions or pleasure experienced when reading a portfolio. For example, does the interplay of your links and graphics make you smile and say that it is a job well done? **Efferent** refers to the information obtained and relayed in a portfolio. It is wise to have others read through your portfolio and share with you the messages your portfolio conveys to them. Read on and investigate more deeply how to apply these two broad terms to the creation of your portfolio.

Aesthetics

The use of the term *aesthetics* in this chapter simply refers to the attractiveness, or the pleasure factor, of your portfolio. Always keep the audience in mind as you design your portfolio. Keep the layout attractive and colorful, while making sure that it does not appear too busy or overcrowded. Consider the captions to use with your photographs. Survey your friends to determine which fonts and font sizes are the easiest to read. Avoid extreme colors that may cause your audience to squint—you want to catch their eye, not give them a headache.

Use an easy-to-follow format to guide the reader through your portfolio in a comfortable manner. Whatever style you choose, we recommend that you include a table of contents. For traditional portfolios, paginate your artifacts, label your sections, and consider using color-coded tabs as guides. For Web portfolios, having clearly labeled links and keywords will create a simple and effective means of reviewing your work. In addition to increasing your audience's incentive to read through your artifacts, this type of organization will also help you refer to specific items during an interview.

There are pros and cons to consider when deciding whether or not to use clear plastic page protectors with your traditional portfolio. They are neat, they keep pages from becoming crumpled, and they eliminate the need to hole-punch important documents. On the other hand, they weigh more and take up more space than do single pages. For Web-based folios, be wary of too much "glitter and glitz," such as dancing clip art and spiraling pointers. Make sure the focus is on the content and not your "technological prowess" (Hill, 2003).

If you include photos, certificates, or other oddly shaped items, you may wish to use a scanner instead of including the actual documents. Using a scanner will allow you to keep your precious documents and give you space to write explanations of the importance of the documents beneath their scanned photos.

Efferent Qualities

The term *efferent* describes how you express and receive information. What information do you wish to convey to your audience? Which artifacts

From the Real World

Creating Web-Based Portfolios

Susan LeMay

Still exuberant from my recent graduation, with my head bursting with thoughts of scaffolding, integrating, and motivating, I set off on a long and arduous journey in search of a teaching job. The most common advice I received was that a candidate needs to stand out from her peers just to get an interview.

I vaguely recalled a story told by a retired principal—one person had made a brochure, introducing himself in a nutshell. Not only did it showcase computer savvy, but it was also smaller than the usual résumé. Due to its difference in size, the principal was inclined to place it on the top of the pile, and soon called him for an interview. So I, too, created a trifold, color brochure. "This," one principal exclaimed, "is fantastic! This really makes you stand out! If only I had a position available!" Not to be discouraged, I began mailing dozens of mini-portfolios, including my brochure, not wanting to leave anything out that might catch the eye of an administrator. After spending my life's savings on postage, I decided to compete with the high-tech, computer literate graduates who were creating e-portfolios as part of their college curriculum. I combined everything onto a CD. As a result, I earned three interviews, with each principal waving my sunflower crested disk like a banner and shouting, "This is what got you in the door!" One uttered that she had never seen anything like it.

When I received a rejection letter stating that the winning candidate was more high-tech, I embraced the constructive criticism and designed a Web site. This, however, proved to be a mistake. In my cover letter, I graciously invited administrators to "please visit my Web site for further information," but few ever did. They seemed to covet the hard copy, the one with the bright sunflowers on the label. Not only did it showcase my computer literacy, but it was also small enough to have to stand out on the top of a pile of résumés.

will need explaining? Which are self-explanatory? Which references will best display your work ethic, student-centered skills, and sense of purpose? Will you section your portfolio according to a certain set of teaching standards, or would you rather name your sections in a more personal, self-evaluative manner? As you view your portfolio, ask yourself what items command attention or are memorable. Ask a friend to critically read your portfolio with an eye to what the portfolio communicates about you. Ask someone who does not know you very well to do the same. If the qualities you wish to convey are not evident according to your reviewers, what can you do to make them stand out?

⚹ Portfolio Types

Traditional Portfolios

One of the comments we often hear from principals and other members of the interview team is that, although the electronic portfolios display great technological skills, they are not necessarily convenient or appropriate tools of evaluation for these busy decision makers. What we understand from this comment is that the interview teams would prefer a more traditional form of portfolio. The term **traditional portfolio** describes portfolios that are published on paper—not online or on CD-ROM. The traditional portfolio tends to be in a binder or accordion file folder, and its table of contents is organized with tabs. Traditional portfolios, like electronic portfolios, have both areas of merit and areas of concern. The traditional portfolios are simpler to use when you wish to display hard copies of certain artifacts or create smaller portable portfolios, but they are also cumbersome. Both in terms of organization and storage, the accumulation of all your artifacts and rationales can quickly become an unwieldy proposition.

Electronic Portfolios—Digital and Web Based

One advancement in the field of portfolio development is the innovative electronic portfolio. An **electronic portfolio** is "a purposeful collection of work, captured by electronic means, that serves as an exhibit of individual efforts, progress, and achievements in one or more areas" (Wiedmer, 1998). **Digital portfolios** may be submitted on disk or on CD-ROM, or may be sent by e-mail as attachments. **Web-based portfolios**, on the other hand, allow viewers to access the information at their leisure whenever they go online. Unlike traditional portfolios, both types of electronic portfolios can be made interactive with the use of PowerPoint, hyperlinks, sound, and video. "An electronic portfolio can be more flexible and dynamic than paper because multimedia provides an adaptable structure to present artifacts that convey the vitality of our profession" (Heath, 2002).

According to Wiedmer (1998), electronic portfolios reflect the depth of involvement of the individual in both selection and design. Additionally, electronic portfolios, because of their ability to transmit vivid images and sounds, can more accurately capture and transmit in attention-getting ways the personality of the candidate.

Most important, creating an electronic portfolio demonstrates your technological skills. Instead of simply commenting on your skills, you are demonstrating the ability to incorporate technology into instruction and relating your willingness to improve these skills as new innovations in technology arise (Georgi & Crowe, 1998; Kilbane & Milman, 2003). You will reveal your ability to meet technology standards, your knowledge of current soft and hardware, your creative vision, and your capability to select worthy artifacts (Wiedmer, 1998). These attributes are an asset to the district and therefore worthwhile to display in your electronic portfolio.

Electronic portfolios may include, but are not limited to, the following types of artifacts:

- Web site including résumé, letters of reference, statement of philosophy
- Video clip of applicant teaching a lesson
- Links to other Web sites where the applicant can be found, such as the sites of other organizations, or newspapers that have articles about the applicant
- PowerPoint presentation of the applicant's strengths and how they will benefit the school district

3.1   Artifact

Susan LeMay has created a Web-based portfolio. On her site she makes her philosophy more engaging with her detailed layout and graphics.

A passing comment, a reassuring smile or hug, or a remarkable person one meets along the way can all influence an individual in ways the other may never realize. In the lives of children, a teacher will be one of the most influential persons she or he will ever meet. Children need to recognize and appreciate their own strengths and talents and find delight in their giftedness and creativity in order to feel successful. Helping them to realize their unique abilities is only one aspect of their lives that my philosophy of education centers on.

As Martin Luther King Jr. stated, "We must remember that intelligence is not enough. Intelligence plus character—that is the goal of the true education." A child's upbringing should include the mind, heart, body, and soul. By implementing diverse methodologies in the classroom, such as cooperative learning groups and creative and critical thinking strategies, I hope to help my students create a repertoire of thinking and reasoning strategies, which can be utilized throughout their lives. My goals are to encourage students:

- To clearly communicate.
- To be creative and innovative.
- To develop the skills and values for lifelong learning.
- To develop an awareness of and a commitment to ethical behavior.

By teaching children to contribute to society, they may also develop an understanding and acceptance of differences in their community, while learning that belonging and being included are important to all persons. Moreover, as technology becomes a focal point in the classroom and at home, children will need greater assistance in keeping up with the social and emotional aspects of their lives, and developing healthy and positive identities. As a teacher, I hope to encourage my students to become successful contributors in an ever-evolving world, and help them build a strong sense of character so that some day they will each be that remarkable person one meets along the way.

- List of applicant's technological abilities, with links to examples of each
- Applicant's teaching certificates, test scores, and other documents that can be scanned into the Web site

Regardless of whether you choose a digital or web-based design, you will need to decide on a format for your table of contents. Will you follow the standard INTASC table of contents, using one folder for INTASC and then one for each of the 10 individual standards? A second option is to show the topic area by folder with your artifacts displayed or linked in each of those individual folders. You should still consider creating the portfolio in such a way that it reflects your personality or philosophy. Will you have key philosophical phrases throughout to tie your portfolio together? For example, do you have favorite quotes about education that you would like to incorporate?

Along with the decisions about setup, Web-based portfolios require you, the author, to decide how best to use the Internet. Will you create a Webquest type of portfolio in which the users will follow links to other sites to learn more about you? If so, do you have a personal home page? Or will you use a Web-based platform (see suggested resources) to help you create your site? Will you send your CD-ROM or Web site address ahead of time with your application and then simply bring a brochure to the interview? Artifact 3.1 shows an example from a Web-based portfolio.

With either digital or Web-based portfolios, you will have many creative issues to address. Digital portfolios require you to choose from specific formats for the table of contents? Will each item in the table have a hyperlink that takes the reader to that area? Will you also have links to Internet sites? How will you display your artifact rationales? What font works best? What about background: Will you have plain and simple stationery, or will you have a more lively sort of wallpaper? Take time to view other Web-based portfolios online. Check with your principals or college career centers to see if they have any digital portfolios that you may view. As you explore the work of others, decide what styles best represent you, your philosophy, and your skills.

For examples of other styles of Web-based portfolios, go to http://www.eduscapes.com/tap/topic82.htm. This Web site provides sample templates and relevant article links.

✄ Considerations

Student teachers and veteran teachers alike may wish to consider using electronic portfolios to effectively communicate their talents, skills, and personalities. Criteria established for evaluating portfolios indicate that portfolios should reflect components of purpose, selectivity, diversity, continuing development, reflection, and collaboration.

References

Georgi, D., & Crowe, J. (1998). Digital portfolios: A confluence of portfolio assessment and technology. *Teacher Education Quarterly, 25*(1), 73–84.

Heath, M. (2002). Electronic portfolios for reflective self-assessment. *Teacher Librarian, 30*(1), 19–23.

Hill, D. M. (2003). E-folio and teacher candidate development. *The Teacher Educator, 38*(4), 256–266.

Kilbane, C. R., & Milman, N. B. (2003). *The digital teaching portfolio handbook*. New York: Allyn & Bacon.

Wiedmer, T. L. (1998). Digital portfolios: Capturing and demonstrating skills and levels of performance. *Phi Delta Kappan, 79*(8), 586–589.

Suggested Resources

Web Sites

This page provides links (without comment) to a variety of teaching portfolios online:

http://www.utep.edu/cetal/portfoli/samples.html

This Web site by Zella M. Boulware, Ed.D., and Dennis M. Holt, Ph.D., of the University of North Florida College of Education and Human Services, Division of Curriculum and Instruction, explains to preservice teachers how to use CD-ROM technology to develop portfolios. Go to:

http://www.unf.edu/~dholt/develop/develop.html

For information on e-portfolios and current research on the topic, visit this link:

http://www.eradc.org

This Web site contains samples of Web-hosted electronic portfolios. There are a variety of samples K–2 and beyond available for you to view. Go to:

Curry.edschool.virginia.edu/edlf/589_004/sample.html

Resources for digital and Web-based portfolios are available, including articles, templates, and samples, at this Web site:

http://www.electricteacher.com/onlineportfolio/articales.htm

Putting It All Together

Using Standards to Construct Your Portfolio

As you design your portfolio, it may help you to structure it according to a specified set of standards. Using standards to construct your portfolio allows the reader to quickly and easily identify the aspects of your teaching ability that he or she is most interested in reviewing. This chapter delineates several national standards programs and also provides information on standards for specialized fields.

✥ The Standards

The two primary organizational structures for portfolios are INTASC and TWS, as outlined below.

Interstate New Teacher Assessment and Support Consortium (INTASC)

The Interstate New Teacher Assessment and Support Consortium (INTASC) has identified 10 standards for what beginning teachers should know, as described in Chapter 1. Briefly, these components include:

1. Knowledge of subject
2. Learning and human development
3. Adapting instruction
4. Strategies
5. Motivation and classroom management
6. Communication skills
7. Planning
8. Assessment
9. Commitment
10. Partnerships (INTASC, 2004)

It is noteworthy to add that the National Council for Accreditation of Teacher Education (NCATE) uses the INTASC standards to evaluate teacher education programs.

Teacher Work Sample (TWS)

Teacher Work Sample (TWS) is a relative newcomer to the arena of teacher assessment. According to

the Renaissance Partnership for Improving Teacher Quality (2002),

> Teacher work samples (TWS) are exhibits of teaching performance that provide direct evidence of a candidate's ability to design and implement standards-based instruction, assess student learning and reflect on the teaching and learning process. Also, teacher work samples are teaching exhibits that can provide credible evidence of a candidate's ability to facilitate learning of all students.

The seven standards for TWS include:

1. Contextual Factors
2. Learning Goals
3. Assessment Plan
4. Design for Instruction
5. Instructional Decision-Making
6. Analysis of Student Learning
7. Reflection and Self-Evaluation

✥ Organizing Your Portfolio in Relation to Standards

It may help you and your prospective employers if you arrange your portfolio according to a set of standards adopted by their school, district, or state. One modification to the following table of contents that you may wish to consider is to cross-reference the artifacts that address more than one standard. For example, lesson plans would be appropriate to include in several areas such as learning and human development, adapting instruction, motivation and classroom management, and planning for INTASC standards. Another example is your participation in community events that benefit children, which may fit under the commitment, partnership, and communication standards.

The following table of contents is based upon the INTASC standards; however, when you organize your portfolio be sure to determine which standards are most often used in your

From the Real World

B. J. Richardson

Considerations when being interviewed:

- Do not hesitate to ask questions about the school and its use of technology, state standards, school improvement, etc.
- Try to be calm and objective. Remember, you are interviewing the school as much as it is interviewing you. Be sure you are comfortable with the things you hear and see.
- Before the interview, ask for information, such as the school report card or the curricular guide. Reference this information during your discussion, but make sure the reference fits the current topic.
- If you are using a portfolio, make sure it contains only those items you wish to accentuate and will utilize. Skipping and skimming are "no-no's." Also be sure you have practiced your delivery of your portfolio with friends or relatives.
- Don't get hung up on the salary schedule or benefits. Do ask about these in a professional growth context.
- Be honest and open.
- Be sure to inquire about extracurricular areas you would like to participate in.
- Don't be afraid to ask about the mentoring program.
- Be yourself.

region. If you are using the TWS, an excellent example of a table of contents can be found at http://soe.cahs.colostate.edu/cttec/teacherwork.html. This site also includes examples for the various standards, as we have done for INTASC.

Suggested Table of Contents Based on INTASC (Artifacts 4.1–4.9

showing examples of various elements of this suggested table of contents follow)

III. **Standard: Adapting Instruction**
   A. Group project completed in your mainstreaming class
   B. Descriptions of curricular modifications you've tried and their outcomes
   C. Reflection on the role you played in an IEP meeting
   D. Letter from parents thanking you for the extra time you put into modifying the social studies test for their child with learning disabilities
   E. Examples of how you make curriculum more challenging for students with gifted abilities
   F. Narrative paper on learning about your students who speak English as a second language (*see Artifact 4.3*)

IV. **Standard: Strategies**
   A. Video of you teaching a lesson
   B. Self-evaluation identifying methods you've found success with and others that still need work (*see Artifact 4.4*)
   C. Narrative descriptions of the methods used by your cooperating teachers
   D. Research project on the battles of controversy between experts in the field of classroom instruction
   E. Rationale for changing cooperative learning groups before mid-semester

V. **Standard: Motivation and Classroom Management**
   A. Letters home updating parents on coming projects and homework
   B. Examples of certificates you've created for achievements such as:
      1. improved behavior
      2. excellent effort
      3. all homework in on time for the month
      4. improved attendance
   D. Copy of classroom assertive discipline plan, including Spooner's positive behavior plan (*see Artifact 4.5*)
      1. rules
      2. consequences
      3. student/teacher-generated reward system
      4. charts
   D. Certificate of completion of special classroom management course, seminar, or workshop
   E. Letters of appreciation from parents grateful for the extra effort you gave to their child with emotional or behavioral problems
   F. Summaries of articles on classroom management and/or motivation

VI. **Standard: Communication Skills** (*see Artifact 4.6*)
   A. Copies of minutes from team meetings showing your participation
   B. Copies of position or persuasive papers you've written
   C. Copies of group projects you've completed, demonstrating your ability to work in a group
   D. Certificates of your technological abilities, including:
      1. word processing
      2. Internet
      3. database
      4. spreadsheets

     5. hyperlinks
     6. digital cameras
     7. scanners
  E. Address of your Web site with hard copies of documents included there
  F. Samples of your best handwriting in a handwritten essay (many districts require this in their employment applications)
  G. A video of you presenting a lesson to a class
  H. PowerPoint presentation of your philosophy of teaching
  I. Photo of a bulletin board created by you and your students as a culminating activity

VII. **Standard: Planning**
  A. Copies of lesson plans from each subject and grade level you've worked with during clinical placements (*see Artifact 4.7*)
  B. Copies of curriculum you've created
  C. Copies of group presentations you've team-taught in your courses
  D. A schedule of the entire school day from your clinical experience
  E. Examples of seating charts you've designed
  F. Scope and sequence of a unit you wish to teach

VIII. **Standard: Assessment** (*see Artifact 4.8*)
  A. Copies of established informal assessment charts you've used, citing authors
  B. Copies of informal assessments you've created, including your rationale
  C. Copies of objective tests you've created
  D. Examples of how you modify assessments for students with special learning needs
  E. Skill inventories you've used or would like to use
  F. Learning modality inventories you've learned how to use
  G. Summaries of articles on multiple intelligences
  H. Papers you've written on multicultural issues in assessment

IX. **Standard: Commitment**
  A. Your statement of beliefs/philosophy of education
  B. Certificates of participation in community events
  C. Articles about your volunteer work with nonprofit groups
  D. Your résumé, focusing on the time you've spent working with children in and out of the school setting

X. **Standard: Partnerships** (*see Artifact 4.9*)
  A. Documentation of the help you provided to coordinate a community volunteer drive for your local public school system
  B. Your written thoughts on a legislative session you attended in your state's capital when they discussed education issues
  C. Letters from your local legislators thanking you for meeting with them to discuss education issues
  D. Minutes from the school board meeting you attended to observe how their decision-making process works
  E. Letters from a parent/teacher organization thanking you for your help
  F. Letters you've written to local businesses suggesting ways that they can participate to help improve public education in your town

4.1　Artifact

Tiffany Gilchrist recently graduated with honors from Northern Illinois University in the College of Education. For her Honors Capstone project, Tiffany created a research-supported first-grade interdisciplinary unit. Included are her introductory and concluding remarks.

Incorporating Children's Literature in the Classroom: A First-Grade Interdisciplinary Unit

Over the last twenty-five years educators have been changing their views on how to teach reading in the classroom. These changes have brought both phonics instruction and whole language curriculum closer together to form a more balanced literacy program. According to Leu and Kinzer (2003), a balanced literacy framework includes:

> a combination of integrated beliefs. You believe that both prior knowledge and decoding components are important, but that each child is likely to have slightly different needs in these areas. You also believe in both student-directed, inductive learning in authentic contexts and teacher-directed, deductive learning in specific skills, depending on individual needs. (p. 85)

Teaching reading through these methods allows all learners in the classroom to be reached on some level. By participating in a variety of activities, readers are learning and are assessed in a multitude of ways. Reading, listening, comprehension, predicting, questioning, and inferring skills are all addressed and further developed.

One important aspect of a balanced reading program is the belief of the teacher. If an educator does not philosophically agree with the method he or she uses to implement the curriculum, the implementation will not be as successful.

Balanced reading instruction is made up of five distinct components: reading aloud, shared reading, guided reading, independent reading, and responding critically and thoughtfully to literature. In a classroom setting it is crucial that all of these elements are included when implementing the reading curriculum in order for a balance to be reached. The following sections will discuss the importance of each of these individual methods as well as provide ideas for putting into practice each method in a classroom environment.

Conclusion

As has been shown, a balanced literacy program is the ideal way to teach reading in the classroom. Students are immersed in reading activities when this type of setup is implemented. Students are exposed to read-alouds that improve their listening skills while fostering a love of books. They participate in shared readings that emphasize enjoying and appreciating the text, guided readings that build confidence in their own reading abilities, and independent readings that make students responsible for their own silent reading comprehension and enjoyment. Extension activities round out the balanced program by allowing the teacher to expand and build upon what the students have just read. It is all of the above components, combined and implemented together, that further the individual growth of each student as a reader.

Each of these separate aspects of the program addresses a different style of reader in the classroom. Both low and high students are able to participate in the curriculum at the same time, each at his or her own individual levels. This is done seamlessly, so that there is no embarrassment to any student in the classroom. Groupings are changed often and based on different aspects for different projects. In this type of literacy environment, students are not only learning from the teacher, but from each other as well. This shared experience of literacy is what makes the balanced approach so beneficial. It makes every member of the class feel like he or she is a member of a reading community, a community that works together to make sure that all its members succeed.

4.2   Artifact

As you read this reflection by Kari Hein-Doege, notice how Kari demonstrates her understanding of the needs of students across age levels.

I believe that from everything I have detailed observing a 3rd-grade classroom and 9th and 11th-grade high school students, I have a good understanding of what I would incorporate. The first would be clear rules and procedures at the beginning of the school year, which I would continue to reinforce throughout the year. It seems that these teachers had very few problems with classroom management because they set the expectations on the very first day.

The second would be to continue my high energy level. I found that with both groups of students, the more the teacher was enthused and actively participating, the more the students were engaged and learning. I also would begin my lessons immediately when class began and end when the bell rang. I would work to establish procedures so that the students would always have a sense of what was coming next, and could move freely with me to that. I don't want to waste so much time transitioning my students from one activity to the next.

The third would be to develop positive relationships with my students and get to know them. It seems that the more you know your students and show an interest in their lives, the more they may become engaged and actively learning.

Fourth, I think it's important to teach from bell to bell and maximize my time with students. And finally, I want to set high expectations for my students. Nothing is impossible. I want to guide each of them to perform to the best of his or her ability. I have seen these things work in both levels of classrooms, and from my observations these are the ideas I would like to incorporate.

4.3   Artifact

As a summer job, Sherri Johnson had the opportunity to teach English to students in China. Here Sherri describes what she learned while visiting the home of one of her students.

Yesterday evening for activities, Sharon and I chose to take some of our kids out for KTV (karaoke). About 13 of my kids wanted to go, and I gave the others a choice between a movie or basketball. The walk to the place took about 15 minutes. By the time we got there we had 45 minutes to sing. We sang mostly American songs with a couple of Chinese songs mixed in. I think that we got the largest party room they had and we packed it with our kids. They had such a great time. (The room came with sugared popcorn and tea.)

After KTV, we took the students back to school and those who lived in town went home. On the way home from school, Bonita and I were walking together. She told me that she would be home alone that night. At our avenue, she asked me to come over to her house. I was not expecting to be asked over, so I was a bit shocked. I had no other plans for the night, so I agreed. It's actually the house of her aunt, uncle, and cousin. I wasn't really expecting anything when I went in. The apartment was on the top floor of the building, no elevator. I was pleasantly surprised about the cleanliness and simplicity of it.

We took a tour of her house and it was so pretty. The bedrooms had just a bed, closet, and desk. There were three bedrooms, a study, a play room, kitchen, dining room, living room, two bathrooms. This apartment had two floors. Bonita and I talked for a bit, I helped her with her English homework, and she fed me oranges. I could tell she really enjoyed having me over. I asked her what she wants to be when she grows up and she tells me a lawyer in the United States. I believe that she will do it someday. She reminds me a lot of what my mom looked like when she was in high school. I told Bonita this and she just smiled.

4.4   Artifact

In the following lesson, Matt Zediker demonstrates his ability to create multilevel, interdisciplinary units.

Spread of Disease

Grades: 5–8

Subjects: Science, Language Arts, Social Studies

Objectives and Illinois State Standards Being Met:

Language Arts: 3A.B—Write to communicate for a variety of purposes.

Science: 12A—Understand the fundamental concepts, principles, and interconnections of the life, physical, and earth/space sciences.

Social Studies: 16.A—Understand events, trends, individuals and movements shaping the expansion era, and how that affected the pioneers.

Goals: Students will learn how easily disease was spread in the western expansion era, and how that affected the pioneers.

Materials: Copies of the definition of *cholera*, and how cholera is contracted, flour, baking soda, vinegar, paper, pencil, diary (with copy of p. 99)

Classroom Management: Whole class participation, also small groups

Introduction: The teacher refers back to the diary that the students have been reading. The teacher then shows a copy of page 99 in the diary. Teacher reads the page aloud and discusses how it refers to the breakout of cholera in St. Louis in the 1800s. Next, the teacher discusses with the class how easy it was to unknowingly contract a disease. Disease was a major reason many pioneers did not make it to their final destinations.

Procedure:

1. Students each choose a canister from the table. Each canister is filled with a combination of flour and/or baking soda. All but one canisters are labeled with numeral 2, 3, or 4; one is labeled with a 1.

2. Tell students that some of them have just contracted a virus. The students with a virus have not been detected, so they do not yet know it they have the disease.

3. Students choose two others to share their "drink" (canister) with. They share by dumping part of their "drink" (canister) into the other person's. If someone comes up to share, they cannot refuse. After everyone has shared their "drinks," they return to their seats.

4. The teacher comes around and pours vinegar into each canister. If the canister contains baking soda, it will foam, indicating the student is "infected." If the canister contains only flour, the vinegar floats on top—the student is not infected.

5. The teacher then posts the list of students who have been infected and the order in which they shared, and the list of students who were not infected and the order in which they shared. The students form groups to try to determine who the original carriers of the disease were (number 1). After they come to a decision, each student looks at the bottom of his or her canister to see who the original carrier is.

Assessment: Using information from the diary page and their own experiences with the project, students write reflective summaries based on what they have learned, and to what extent disease affected the pioneers.

4.5   Artifact

This behavior management plan initiated for all students in his classroom reflects Eric Spooner's understanding of his students' needs and goals.

Positive Behavior Plan

I. *Pins*
   A. Each student has a plastic-strip row on the Blue Chart.
      1. Names at the left end identify the rows.
      2. *Pins* are clipped over the plastic strips as they are earned.
   B. Students earn *Pins* for positive behavior:
      1. following instructions the first time said,
      2. behaving in line as we travel,
      3. moving from center to center quickly and quietly,
      4. putting away supplies when asked,
      5. sitting in his or her seat through breakfast,
      6. cleaning up after breakfast,
      7. behaving during opening ceremonies, or
      8. special acts of kindness.
   C. Once earned, *Pins* cannot be taken away.
   D. When lining up to travel:
      1. the student currently having the most *Pins* is Line-Leader, and
      2. the student with the second most *Pins* is the Caboose.
   E. At the right end of the row is the student's daily *Pin* goal.

II. *Penn Bucks*
   A. The student with the most *Pins* gets a *Penn Buck* at:
      1. lunchtime, and
      2. the end of the day.
   B. A *Penn Buck* is also awarded:
      1. each time a student achieves his or her daily goal, or
      2. when an adult sees special behavior.
   C. *Penn Bucks* are kept behind the names on the Blue Chart.

III. Discipline
   A. Inappropriate behavior will be disciplined immediately.
   B. Two to three minutes in time-out for most offenses.
      1. Time starts when student is quiet in time-out.
      2. Teacher or TAs will discuss the rules with student.
      3. Time in time-out is lengthened in 1-minute increments for:
         a. throwing fits and acting-out while in time-out, and
         b. resisting going to time-out.
   C. Two to three minutes of floor-time for:
      1. more serious offenses, or
      2. group offenses.
      3. Time starts when student is quietly standing.
      4. Teacher or TAs will discuss the rules with student.
      5. Time at floor-time is lengthened in 1-minute increments for:
         a. throwing fits and acting-out while at floor-time, or
         b. resisting going to floor-time.

4.6 Artifact

In the following letter, Melissa Denna describes an exciting new home-school connection project to her students' parents. This project demonstrates how Melissa and her colleague use a variety of resources to involve and empower parents.

Dear Parents,

In response to our application for a grant, we are fortunate to have received money from the Summit City Education Foundation to purchase two digital cameras. Our plan for these cameras is to put them into the hands of our students and their families in order to explore and learn about the likenesses and differences among different communities. By the time our students leave third grade we would like them to have a clear understanding of the meaning of community, the differences among rural, urban, and suburban communities, and their responsibility toward community. In order to accomplish this, we would like to involve the students in a hands-on project. The project will include taking pictures of a variety of communities, interviewing community members, and student research.

In order for this project to be a success and for our students to receive optimal learning, we are asking that families utilize these digital cameras when taking a ride in the country, and when visiting different cities and suburban communities. After your family has made a plan to visit one or more of these communities, please contact us so we may supply you with one of the digital cameras and the directions for its use. If you would prefer to use your own camera, please have your pictures transferred to a CD so they may be included in the class project.

We have spoken to your child about this project and plan to explain in further detail. If you have further questions, please contact us for clarification.

Thanks for your continued support,
Mrs. Reyes and Miss Denna

4.7 Artifact

In the following reflection, Tamara Simms describes her attempts to implement a variety of teaching strategies for an outdoor education unit.

The first outdoor education lesson I delivered was the solar wood-burning activity. The students learned about solar energy, the process of magnification, and how converging lenses work. The children were so excited about burning their initials into blocks of wood! Thankfully, the weather and the sun cooperated—we spent three consecutive afternoons outdoors. I borrowed small magnifying glasses from the other fourth-grade teacher. The students had a somewhat difficult time starting the process because the lenses may have been too small. However, the second day of this activity, many students brought larger magnifying glasses from home. They were able to burn their initials more quickly and shared their lenses with the other students.

The second outdoor education lesson I delivered focused on animal habitats. The students chose an animal they liked and wanted to research. We spent about four days finding information about the animals in the school library using magazines and books, at the computer lab surfing the Internet, and using encyclopedias from the classroom. These students have never truly researched anything before. I had a hard time keeping them on task—they all wanted to share their interesting findings with me! I then instructed them on how to create a formal three-paragraph paper. This part was the most challenging—again, many of the students have never written a paper like this. The students then constructed habitat dioramas using shoeboxes. They were so creative with their materials and displays—I was extremely impressed and very proud of them all! Each student then delivered a three-minute presentation describing their dioramas and sharing information about their animal. Overall, this project was my favorite of all the things I did during my student teaching.

4.8   Artifact

Rubrics are popular and effective forms of assessment that help teachers be objective and help students self-monitor. See what you think of the following oral presentation rubric from Nancy Gray's interdisciplinary unit. Are the skills measurable, and are the criteria clear?

Oral Presentation Rubric

	0–1 points	2 points	3–4 points	5 points
Content	Subject not clear; information does not support topic	Subject clear, but few supporting details	Subject clear and many supporting details	Abundance of interesting details that support topic
Organization	Presentation disjointed	Concepts loosely connected	Generally well organized with a couple transitions	Well-developed introduction, body of information, and conclusion
Speaking skills	No eye contact; delivery too fast or too slow; monotone	Little expression; some eye contact	Articulate but not practiced enough	Articulate, poised, confident, delivery; good eye contact
Audience response	Audience lost interest and could not follow topic	Audience was interested half the time	Presented information with some interesting "twists"	Held audience's attention throughout
Additional inclusions	No, or incomplete, science/social science information	Included 2 pieces of information related to science/social science	Included 3 pieces of information related to science/social science	Included 2 pieces of information related to science and 2 to of social science
Points received				

4.9   Artifact

Notice the brevity of Erica's letter of introduction to her students' parents. What other information can you include in such a letter while still keeping it short and to the point?

To the parents of Mrs. Watson's class:

My name is Erica Brittain. I will be student teaching in Mrs. E-Yung Park's fifth-grade classroom until December. I am a student at Northern Illinois University and will be earning my bachelor's degree in elementary education in December. I look forward to working with the students in my class. I would like to wish you and your children much success this school year.

    Sincerely,
    Erica Brittain

✶ Organizing Your Portfolio According to Teacher Work Sample

This methodology encourages the preservice teacher to demonstrate competence in seven key areas through written descriptions of experiences and decisions made during the execution of a series of lessons or a unit plan. Teacher and student products are incorporated as evidence of the learning that took place during the assignment. Similar to the INTASC artifacts, **Teacher Work Sample (TWS)** is accomplished through authentic assessment of your teaching by guiding you through the process of assessment before, during, and after instruction, focusing on your knowledge of your students and community, and leading you to an in-depth reflection of your classroom skills. As the graphic below presents, TWS is concerned with the demonstration of how your knowledge and skills impact the education of your students. Throughout your portfolio, remember to demonstrate these three fundamental areas (Colorado State University):

> Candidate → Candidate Use of → Effect on Learning
> Knowledge   Knowledge in Practice   in P–12 Students

I. Setting and Context

a. Explore the relationship between the community and the school. Describe the culture that is evident in the school and the community at large. This should include the support structure that exists and the use of parents or volunteers in the classroom.

b. Research the demographics of the school and analyze how you used this information to your advantage in instructional planning. You may wish to use documentation from the school directly in this section to support your ideas.

c. Prior to teaching, observe the students in your classroom as a sociologist would do for an experiment. You may view this assignment as participant-observer research to discover the preferred learning styles that your students exhibit and what skills they still need to develop to meet the goals you will establish for your lesson or unit. Record this information in paragraph format for the TWS.

II. Learning Goals

a. Provide a brief description of the lesson or unit you will be teaching.

b. Explain in more detail the implications of this lesson or unit from both a world viewpoint and a personal viewpoint which will speak to the significance of why you planned this topic and the appropriateness for the students. This may also be viewed as a justification for why you are doing what you have planned within the lesson or unit. After discussing the viewpoints, include a rationale for the plan based on the viewpoints and the challenge it provided for the students.

c. Give an accounting of the national, state, and/or local standards that will be addressed in the lesson or unit plan. These are critical for the school to represent and will provide you with a vehicle to present your understanding of the standards and their significance in your planning. You may wish to delve in to further detail in how the standards will be addressed through the variety of your teaching methods and curriculum that you have planned for the students.

III. Assessment Plan

a. Remember those goals you just finished writing about in section 2? In section 3, discuss the method(s) that you used to make sure your students mastered the skills contained within those standards. Provide a copy of a rubric or other assessment measures you will use during the unit. Quality over quantity is still important in TWS as it is in INTASC. Do not include every assessment tool, merely provide examples that show your best quality work in this area. Measures of assessment for prelearning, during the instructional phase and mastery should be included in your explanation or examples.

b. It is very important that you discuss any adaptations or provisions you have made in your lesson or unit to meet the needs of all students in your classroom. This can be accomplished through differentiation in your plan, incorporating universal instructional design, or other means of tweaking the lesson so that all learners had exit mastery of the goals and objectives you established for the lesson or unit. [Review Chapter 6 for a discussion of differentiation.]

IV. Design for Instruction

a. Briefly discuss your objectives and the connection to standards.

b. Provide a timeline of the lesson or unit to demonstrate the overall structure of the plan. This should be brief in description as you will provide a more detailed description later in this section.

c. In paragraph form, provide a walk-through of the lesson or unit, highlighting the variety of instruction and cooperative learning strategies that you presented to the students. Refer back to section 1 as you give an accounting of your strategies and content that will speak to the relevance for those that you chose based on the contextual factors of your classroom. It is recommended that you use a minimum of three strategies for a lesson, with at least one of these being a cooperative learning methodology. Be sure that your presentation in this section demonstrates a cohesive lesson or unit and not merely a jumble of activities.

d. You must include any adaptations or accommodations that you made for exceptional learners in your classroom. Consider any enrichment activities that you provided for the gifted students in your classroom or demonstrate your competency in this area through a differentiated lesson plan.

e. Technology is an important part of the classroom and your competence in using and intertwining its use in your lesson is critical. Describe how you incorporated various technologies into the lesson that you used and that the students had an opportunity to utilize to meet the objectives of the lesson.

V. Instructional Decision Making

a. As the lesson progressed, discuss how you gauged whether your students were understanding and learning the material. If the students were struggling to follow along or keep pace with the lesson, describe the adjustments you made to accommodate the learners or what adjustments you made to the overall lesson.

b. Any adjustments made to the lesson must be in line with your objectives. It is critical to discuss the adjustments and the connection to the standards.

VI. Analysis of Student Learning

Using graphs and charts will be critical in this section to demonstrate your assessment knowledge, as well as your technical proficiency.

a. How well did your students perform in the lesson or unit? By analyzing the pre- and postassessments, you should have a clear picture of the growth that occurred in the students' knowledge through your instruction. Examine those students who show advancement in knowledge as well as those whose individual gains were not significant. What is the difference between these students? What could you do differently to effectively reach the students that did not progress as far as others?

b. Review the relationship between your objectives and your assessments. Did you actually assess your students on the material you stressed in your lesson? Do the assessments show the learning that may or may not have occurred during the lesson? Did the students master the skills identified in the standards?

c. Describe the assessments and the benefits of each in relation to multiple intelligences and your students learning habits (from section 1). Which assessments did your students prefer and on which did they perform their best? Discuss your use of traditional, authentic, and self and peer assessments throughout the lesson or unit.

d. What grading criteria did you establish and how did you determine scores? Was your scoring and assessment tool(s) reliable? Feasible? Appropriate?

VII. Reflection and Self-Evaluation

a. As you complete various stages of the lesson or unit, reflect on the progress of your teaching, student learning, and the lesson or unit itself. What went well? What did the students struggle to understand? What did you learn about yourself, your students, and the teaching process?

b. Examine how your classroom management effected the instruction of your lesson or unit. How does your philosophy tie into this area? What would you do to improve student cooperation or what worked well in motivating students to participate in your lesson?

c. How did this experience enhance or affect your personal and professional goals? What are you eager to do the next time you teach a lesson or unit? What are you interested in learning to increase your skills in the classroom? What professional development will you seek for the future?

d. Were you able to maintain alignment among the goals, your instruction, and the assessments that you chose? Were you on target with the abilities of your students? Were you able to accomplish all the goals and standards that you set out to complete? Will you make any adjustments in the future?

✄ Considerations

Whether you create a portfolio based on INTASC, TWS, or some other set of standards, what you create will be a fine example of your knowledge and skills as a teacher. The portfolio will be available to parents, administration, and other teachers for ideas and insight into your teaching style and competencies. Keep your portfolio updated for when your administrator comes to visit your classroom. Using the TWS format is a simple visual representation for your principal to review your progress during your early years in the classroom. This type of reflective process is also beneficial practice if you decide to pursue National Board Certification.

One reason to maintain a portfolio is to demonstrate that your knowledge of issues, such as goals and standards, is current. By organizing your portfolio according to a set of standards, you will convey your interest in helping your school district and your students meet standards, and will also show your involvement with educational organizations.

References

Colorado State University, Department of Technology. Retrieved from

http://soe.cahs.colostate.edu/cttec/pdf/ TeacherWork%20Sample.pdf

Martin, D. B. (1999). *The portfolio planner: Making professional portfolios work for you.* Upper Saddle River, NJ: Merrill.

Maxwell, M. (1997). *Improving student learning skills, a new edition.* Clearwater, FL: H & H Publishing.

Renaissance Partnership for Improving Teacher Quality. (2002). *Teacher work sample.* Retrieved from

http://fp.uni.edu/itq/RTWS/

Suggested Resources

Web Sites

For details and descriptions of the INTASC standards, go to:

http://www.ccsso.org/intaspub.html

For more information on TWS and useful examples, go to:

http://fp.uni.edu/itq/RTWS/

For more information on National Association for the Education of Young Children (NAEYC) standards, go to:

http://www.naeyc.org

For more information or to request a copy of the standards for your specific disciplines, call 1-800-22-TEACH, or go to the National Board for Professional Teaching Standards Web site:

http://www.nbpts.org

For more information on the National Council for Accreditation of Teacher Education (NCATE), go to:

http://ncate.org/

For more information on integrated reading and writing standards, go to:

http://www.ncte.org/ or http://www.ira.org/

Displaying Classroom Management in Your Portfolio

Whether you are a first-year educator about to embark on the marvelous journey of teaching second graders, or a veteran educator beginning your 20th year of enlightening high schoolers, you need to have a **classroom management plan.** Your plan will include your expectations of behavior, rules, planned consequences for following (or not following) the rules, and a record-keeping method of monitoring such compliance or lack of compliance. In addition to the plan itself, there are many other important classroom management issues for you to address. Communicating with students, parents, colleagues, and administrators requires insight, organization, tact, clarity, and competence. The physical arrangement of your classroom, too, provides many challenges and can often either lead to or prevent disciplinary problems.

INTASC: Standard 5—Motivation and Classroom Management

Teaching Standard

Artifacts described in this chapter would be placed in standard 5 to demonstrate your knowledge of management, collaboration and connections within and outside of the classroom. Choose your artifacts to display the variety of skills you bring to the table within the domain of management and parental involvement.

TWS: Contextual Factors

Teaching Standard

Management includes knowledge of your classroom and the students in your care. How you conduct your classroom has direct implications on your instructional planning and the variety of approaches you will use in presenting your lessons. This information should be discussed in the first link, folder, or tab in your portfolio.

✖ Communication and Management Styles

Just as there are many variations of educational philosophies, so too are there many variations of classroom management styles. Even in your earliest clinical experiences, you will be experimenting to find your own style of communicating and enforcing your expectations. Effective classroom management means making modifications for students with special needs; for example, if Donita learns better by working in a quiet place, she will benefit from your allowing her to move to a corner to work. By allowing Donita to move, you are also practicing preventive classroom management. Talk to your cooperating teachers and your instructors to find out the ways that they use preventive classroom management. In your portfolio, include your written observations of these professionals' methods and your ideas for methods you would like to try.

Michael Kosky observed a secondary physical education classroom at an alternative school for special education students. Read his reflection to discover how one school uses communication and management together.

> Since this is an alternative school, they have some built-in systems that should help in classroom management. They devised a behavior sheet that utilizes a point system based on successfully meeting certain criteria. The students have this sheet filled out every class, and by accumulating points, they move up levels and earn more rewards. It is an excellent system if the teachers are very clear about how the student will earn or lose points, and if the student buys into it. I thought the PE teacher utilized it very effectively. She would go through the sheet with students and explain their scores to

From the Real World

Creating a Welcoming Classroom Environment

Julie Johnson

The first thing that students will see when they walk in the classroom is a smiling, cheerful teacher! By greeting my students as they enter the room, I hope to set a positive tone for the rest of the day, and I hope to make each student feel welcomed and important. The desks will be arranged in a horseshoe formation in order to create a sense of classroom community. There will also be exciting bulletin board displays that go along with our teamwork theme. I believe if the students feel they are part of a team (community), they will feel more comfortable participating in the classroom. . . . Last, I will make sure that the room remains well organized and that everything is clearly labeled. I believe that organization and structure help students feel comfortable in their surroundings.

In order to help my students see the value of learning, I will try to make it clear that each student is responsible for his or her own success and failure in life. My goal will be to help them understand that the extent of success is determined by how much effort and hard work they are willing to exert. My main point here will be that you are not going to get the things that you want out of life by sitting back and waiting for them to happen. You must exert some effort, and must sometimes do things that are a little difficult, like schoolwork.

them. The students would try to negotiate with her when they felt they should score higher. She would listen and sometimes keep it the same and other times change. It was not that the students were manipulating her; she was paying attention to how the students approached her about it. She appeared to see the big picture with the students and work with them.

The junior high teacher also utilized the point system, but she was not as structured with it as the PE teacher. She would take away points for poor behavior, but would also give points and compliment the students for positive behaviors. The problem was that her points system was so nominal it had little or no meaning to the students. There were points coming and going so fast that the students could not always get an accurate count of how many they had. It appeared to me that the students were confused and more disagreements would occur because of it.

Sometimes utilizing proactive communication is just plain fun. There are myriad reproducible resources available in teacher stores, catalogs, and online. One excellent resource is the *Classroom Teacher's Survival Guide: Practical Strategies, Management Techniques, and Reproducibles for New and Experienced Teachers* (Partin, 2005).

In the following reflection, Susan LeMay describes her observation of a terrific use of pocket charts to monitor students' behavior.

I was serving as a long-term substitute in a first- and second-grade multiage class and the teacher before me had a great behavior plan. Using a 30-pocket chart, she filled each pocket with the same six cards: white, blue, green, orange, red, and yellow. Each pocket had a student's name on the front. Each time the student misbehaved, he or she pulled one card and put it behind the others. Each color that was showing had a consequence. White meant you haven't pulled any, blue and green were just warnings.

5.1   Artifact

In the following reflection, Kari Hein-Doege relates her observations of a high school English class and the professional relationship that the cooperating teacher had established with the students.

Sara had a commanding presence and talked loudly and directly when she needed their attention; she also could be soft spoken and sweet when talking with a student one-on-one. Her procedure for students to turn in their work was excellent. She had bins marked for each period, and students were expected to just turn things in. They also knew where to look to find out their evening homework assignment. I think the biggest reward she offered the students was her sense of humor. She had even more energy at the end of the day than at the beginning. She attributed that to students really needing her high energy to keep them focused and on task at the end of the day.

The students seemed quite respectful toward Sara and did not give her a hard time. She taught from bell to bell, and students worked all the way through. If a student did goof off a bit, all she would have to do was look at the student and say his or her name, and then the situation would be resolved.

It seemed as if Sara had probably done such a good job with rules and procedures at the beginning of the year that she had very few problems when I observed the classroom. Again, her body language was open, expressive, and inviting to students. She complimented them and offered good feedback. The climate of her classroom was very positive. Sara stood in the hallway welcoming students as they walked in.

I have a good understanding of the strategies I would incorporate in my own classroom. The first would be clear rules and procedures. It seemed that this teacher had few problems from a classroom management standpoint because she set the expectations from the very first day forward. The second would be to continue my high energy level. I also would begin my lessons immediately and end when the bell rang. I don't want to waste so much time transitioning my students from one activity to the next. The third would be to develop positive relationships with my students and get to know them. Nothing is impossible. I want to guide each of them to do their very best.

Orange meant you missed ½ of your recess (at this point, I have them write a letter home telling why the three cards were pulled) and red was the whole recess. Yellow was a conference with Mom and Dad, which I had to do one time. As the students in this school progress from one grade level to the next, they have the same behavior plan. For Grades 3 and 5, however, students write the reason on the card, place the card on the teacher's desk, and the misbehavior is logged by the teacher on a form for conferences. During the first week I was there, the same two children were pulling five or six cards every day. A month later they rarely had to pull one. Both got award certificates at the end of the month for being nice to their classmates!

Communicating with Students

We cannot overestimate the value of communicating positive expectations to students, nor can we exaggerate the benefits of giving specific feedback to students (see Artifact 5.1). You may be asked to create a discipline plan for your student teaching experience. Word it in a positive, proactive way, make it attractive and simple to read, and copy it for your portfolio.

Read the following classroom rules implemented by Patty Rieman in her class for students with behavior disorders. Note that the word *not* is never used; it is much more effective to state your expectations positively. Most experts suggest that classroom rules be simply stated and number only a few. It is best to have the rules in mind when you start the school year, but you should still discuss them with your students. Students often have good ideas and enjoy sharing in decision making. When they feel ownership in the rules, students are more likely to help enforce them.

Classroom Rules

1. Do no harm.
2. Respect others' property, space, and feelings.
3. Come on time and prepared to work.
4. Ask for help appropriately and when needed.
5. Instead of "I can't," say, "I will try, but I need help."
6. Follow all school rules.

Communicating with Colleagues and Administrators

Your colleagues and administrators, too, are impacted daily by your classroom management style. In elementary school, or, in fact, at any level of school, parents and students will compare your classroom management strategies to those of your colleagues.

It is important to combine your individual style with a consistent message conveyed by the staff as a whole. In middle school or high school, your team or department may have a policy regarding discipline. When you apply for a teaching position, ask for a copy of the student handbook. Consider placing in your portfolio a copy of the school's mission statement and/or your team or departmental policy. Comment on this artifact and state how you plan to enforce these beliefs. (See Artifact 5.2.)

 ## 5.2   Artifact

The following mission statement and behavior management model are found in a middle school student handbook. How would you express your plan to uphold and enforce these ideals?

Mission Statement

The staff at Jones Middle School is committed to establishing and maintaining an equitable and dynamic educational experience designed to meet the unique physical, emotional, and social needs of the adolescent learner. We realize that a strong home-school-community relationship that emphasizes good communication is crucial to the successful completion of our mission.

Behavior Management

(After an introductory paragraph, the following expectations and consequences are delineated.)

Students are expected to:

1. Follow directions the first time they are given.
2. Listen respectfully when others are speaking.
3. Work in class without disturbing others.
4. Respect others' rights, feelings, and property.
5. Conduct themselves in a manner that promotes safety for all.

Consequences for misbehavior include:

1. Warning
2. Classroom detention with teacher, with parent or guardian contact (written/phone)
3. Formal after-school detention with parent or guardian contact (written/phone)
4. Team meeting with the student
5. Team meeting with the student and parent/guardian
6. Referral to the principal for further disciplinary action, including suspension

Severe Clause: Students may be referred to the office at any time for severe disruptions.

Communicating through High-Quality Correspondence

Many educators have left themselves open to unfavorable criticism by unwittingly sending out letters, permission forms, and newsletters that are riddled with errors in punctuation and grammar. These poorly worded, ill-conceived missives can often be the undoing of an otherwise competent teacher—what

5.3   Artifact

While student teaching, Erica Brittain was responsible for writing and publishing the weekly classroom newsletter. Notice the skills Erica shows in this artifact—use of technology, articulation of thoughts, organization of information, and ability to use the writing process to create error-free documents.

Miss Brittain's

Week of November 15

Dear Parents,

I hope everyone enjoyed the extra-long weekend! It was really nice to talk with all the parents during parent–teacher conferences. I think everyone's doing great!

There is a holiday collection for the South Suburban Crisis Center that is being held at school. The student council is in charge of collecting new items from people willing to donate. If you are interested, please send **new** items to school with your child such as blankets, coats, clothing, toys, etc. The collection is being held from now until December 10.

We just received the information about the DARE graduation. It will be held on **December 6,** at 6:30 pm. The ceremony will be held in Memorial's gym. More information will be given closer to the date.

Last week we read the story *Island of the Blue Dolphins.* We will continue to read this story this week, since last week was shortened. This is also the last reading story in the theme, so we will move on to Theme 3 next week. The students will be taking a Theme 2 posttest and a Theme 3 pretest toward the end of this week.

The students really seem to be enjoying science. Since the science is so hands-on, the children are engaged in what they are learning. This week we will continue to create different landforms.

Remember to keep up your outside reading requirements. There are only a few students with at least one sticker. Keep reading! Enjoy your week! ☺

Miss Brittain

This Week's Agenda

Monday: The students will work on a science investigation.

Tuesday: We will reread the story *Island of the Blue Dolphins.*

Wednesday: The students will be learning about making inferences and we will play a grammar alphabet game.

Thursday: Theme 2 posttest will be given.

Friday: There will be a cumulative review and a spelling test. We will also be attending a Lewis and Clark musical at 10:45 am.

Student of the Week

Marquis
Tenisha

parent or principal wants such a role model for his or her children and students? By including high-quality, error-free examples of correspondence in your portfolio, you will immediately alleviate this common administrative concern. Artifact 5.3 shows a well-written classroom newsletter.

Connecting with Parents

One of the strongest proactive classroom management tools is the practice of working effectively with parents. Not only are parents the most vital link in students' educational chains, but parents also know their children better than anyone else. In her comments on fostering home–school connections, Pamela Farris (2005) notes the following two guidelines: (1) Respect students as part of the team—if they feel ownership in their learning and decisions, they will help foster better home–school communication. (2) Ensure parental involvement whenever possible. Research suggests that students with involved parents achieve more than those whose parents are not involved. This is particularly problematic after students complete their primary grades. Sometimes parents may feel that because they are not well educated, they have nothing to offer. Regardless of level of education, parents' involvement does positively impact their children's learning (see Artifacts 5.4 through 5.6).

5.4   Artifact

The following letter of thanks was written by Melissa Denna to the mother of one of her students. How does Melissa's letter relate to the above guidelines from Farris?

Dear Mrs. Smith,

I wanted to take this opportunity to thank you for all of the time and effort you have put into making my student teaching experience rewarding. While I do not have children of my own, I realize working parents have a very demanding lifestyle. The supplies you have given me have helped provide the students with the most authentic lessons possible. Let it not go unsaid that the Valentine's Day party was a success because of your creativity and generosity.

I can only hope that I have a classroom full of parents like you when I begin the school year with my own class. Please accept this letter on behalf of the entire class and me; we value your hard work!

Sincerely,

Miss Melissa Denna

5.5   Artifact

Alton Rollerson, a teacher in an urban district, reflects on the vital relationship between parents and teachers.

After teaching, I realize that a teacher cannot fully give the student everything he or she needs without the continued reinforcement of the parents at home. There is only so much a teacher can do in a school day, but once the student leaves the school, he or she is under the parent or guardian's care. If they are not on the same page with the teachers, the student might not get a complete education.

5.6   Artifact

Melissa Denna wrote the following "Help Wanted" ad to encourage the home–school connection.

HELP WANTED!

MOMS   DADS   GRANDPARENTS

We need volunteers to do some simple jobs throughout the school year. Most of these jobs take place right in your home! The jobs range from preparing book orders to labeling books. Each job that is sent home will include a set of directions and supplies that you will need to complete the job. The work is rewarding and fun!

We appreciate your time and effort. Thank you for your assistance!

Sincerely,

Miss Denna's Class

_____Yes! I will help the class. Please send home things that I can assist with.

_____Yes! I will help the class. Please send home things that I can assist with. I am also willing to assist at school during the school day.

_____Sorry, I am unable to help at this time.

_____Your Name

✄ Seating Charts and Floor Plans

As you become familiar with both your learning and teaching style and the needs and preferences of your students, you will often find yourself looking critically at your classroom layout. Decisions such as whether to use rows of desks, pods or clusters of desks, or tables and chairs should be based on whether students will benefit from being together or whether they will be more comfortable and able to attend by sitting alone. Additionally, components out of your control such as electrical outlets, climate control, doors, windows, lights, and bulletin boards must all be taken into account when you are designing the layout of your room (Artifact 5.7).

In your portfolio, include a floor plan of your classroom and write a rationale for the organization. If you have not yet had the opportunity to rearrange a classroom, observe several styles of classrooms and take notes on what you think are the best ideas. Draw diagrams to help you remember these ideas.

✄ Case Studies

Every teacher has at least one student for whom he or she wishes to find a magic "cure." The student may be brilliant but lacking in motivation, be reluctant to speak but a gifted writer, be better one-on-one than in groups, or be

5.7   Artifact

As you read Tamara Simms's floor plan and reflection, notice how she displays her values and philosophy within her comments. Both what you choose to say and what you choose to omit relay messages.

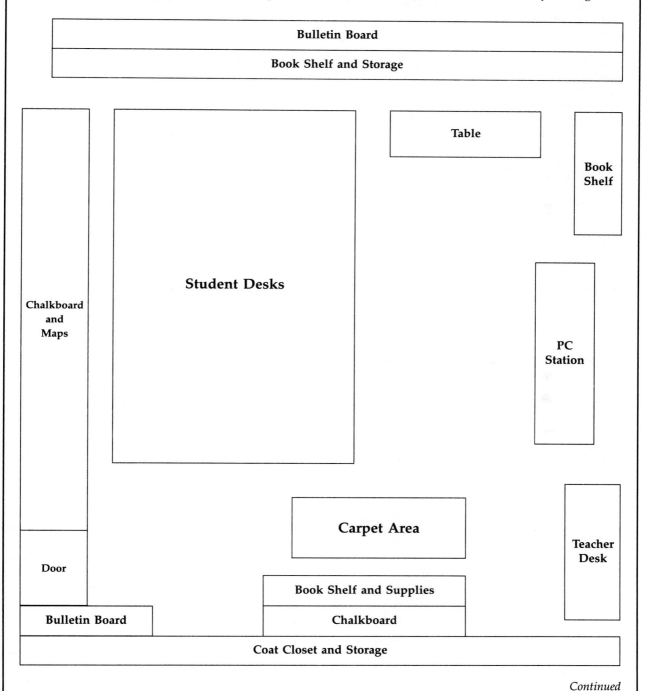

Continued

5.7   Artifact   *Continued*

The school I student taught in was built over 100 years ago in the heart of a rural, midwestern industrial community. This quaint building has all of the "old school" charm and character of a bygone era—hardwood floors, 12-foot ceilings, and water-stained plaster walls veined with the signs of time and settlement. Each classroom contains a large built-in coat closet and storage area. The chalkboards are only 2 feet high but span nearly the entire perimeter of the room. Rather than being a contemporary ranch-style structure, this school was constructed three stories high. There is no elevator to take you up or down—stairs (and lots of them!) are the only way to move between levels. There is no air conditioning and rarely does the furnace provide a comfortable 72 degrees in the dead of winter. But that's OK—the warmth comes from the hustle and bustle of active teaching and learning which is evident in every classroom.

The student population is roughly 70% Hispanic with about the same percentage on the free/reduced lunch program. Needless to say, this district faces more important challenges than faulty plumbing. In the past, the school had been placed on a "watch list" for not making Adequate Yearly Progress in the areas of reading and math. After reevaluation of the curriculum and teacher methodology, standardized scores have greatly improved and they are now making tremendous AYP! The sights and sounds of this building in much needed repair are apparent, yet oddly enough, it does not interfere with the overall quality of the teaching and learning process. Sure, the freight train intersection is just across the street, the old fluorescent bulbs occasionally flicker, and the

ancient clocks have some difficulty keeping time, but student attendance is high and teacher enthusiasm is abundant.

I also student taught in a very affluent western suburb of Chicago. Property taxes are sky-high in this area so each child has immediate access to high-technology resources, school lunches are more like seven-course meals (no dried-up fish sandwiches in this cafeteria!), and teachers are paid the best salary in the state. However, these students do not display the same respect for education as do their lower-class counterparts. Their value is placed on extracurricular experiences—two-week-long soccer camps, guest speakers who serve as CEO for multimillion-dollar corporations, and global travel with their dual-professional-career parents. They seem to challenge the teachers with their false sense of heightened knowledge—"What could you possibly teach me when I have already done and seen more than you may ever in your lifetime?"

Although I loved the numerous conveniences of working within such a wealthy district, I have come to realize that I actually prefer the challenges found within the underprivileged school. Students come daily knowing they want (and need) to learn. These children hang on your every word, as if you hold the magic key to unlock the door to opportunity. Teaching and learning in this school is truly reciprocal—I honestly believe my students taught me more than I taught them in that short semester. I have an interview scheduled next week with this school's principal. Hopefully, I will be asked to join their family and be given the key to my door of opportunity.

an incredible distraction to others whenever present. There is a key to success for every student. It is always the goal that classroom teachers find and use the key in time to make a difference.

One valuable portfolio artifact is a narrative case study of a particular student. The first step is to either obtain parental permission to use the student's name and experiences, or take precautions to protect the confidentiality rights of that student. Next, observe and document several sessions with the student. Note times of day, subjects, types of behavior, and what appears to trigger the behavior. After identifying the behavior, settings, and possible reasons for the behavior, describe how you plan to help the student and your rationale. The subsequent step will be describing the outcome of your intervention. Finally, follow up with more observations after the new behaviors have become routine.

✖ Considerations

Parents often cite school discipline as one of their greatest concerns, and principals have the unfortunate task of dismissing otherwise bright and talented educators because of their inability to effectively create a positive learning environment. Classroom management should be used as a proactive, preventative tool. It is important that your portfolio demonstrate your ability to anticipate problems, be sensitive to students' needs, and keep parents, administrators, and colleagues well informed. You have already seen sample letters, contact forms, and school discipline plans. What other items might display your knowledge of classroom management?

References

Farris, P. J. (2005). *Language Arts: Process, product, and assessment.* 4th ed. Long Grove, IL: Waveland Press.

Partin, R. (2005). *Classroom teacher's survival guide: Practical strategies, management techniques, and reproducibles for new and experienced teachers.* San Francisco: Jossey-Bass.

Suggested Resources

Print

Kidder, T. (1998). *Among schoolchildren.* Boston: Houghton Mifflin.

Paley, V. P. (1992). *You can't say, you can't play.* Cambridge, MA: Harvard University Press.

Wong, H. K., & Wong, R. T. (2004). *The first days of school.* Mountain View, CA: Harry K. Wong Publications.

Web Sites

The Really Big List of Classroom Management Resources Web page:

http://drwilliampmartin.tripod.com/classm.html

For *ProTeacher* Archive, Community Pages, and Behavior Management Survey, go to:

http://www.proteacher.com/030000.shtml

For tips and specific how-to's from middle school teachers across the country, go to:

http://www.pacificnet.net/~mandel/ClassroomManagement.html

For *Education World's* links to archives of classroom management articles, go to:

http://www.education-world.com/a_curr/archives/classmanagement.shtml

For teaching strategies on classroom management from the Center for Research on Learning and Teaching (CRLT) at the University of Michigan, go to:

http://www.crlt.umich.edu/crlttext/tscmtext.html

Presenting Lesson Plans and Curricular Modifications

INTASC Standards:

Teaching Standard

In this chapter, focus on standards 1–8. Lesson planning and curricular modifications

TWS:

Teaching Standard

Focus on Design for Instruction, Instructional Decision Making, and Assessment Plan.

✄ The Importance of Planning

One of the most powerful adages about teaching is that the best form of classroom management is a well-organized, engaging, relevant, challenging, and attainable curriculum. The longer you teach, the better you will be able to judge the prior knowledge of your students, the appropriateness of the curriculum, and the amount of time to allow for lessons and activities. However, as a preservice teacher, you do not yet have as rich an array of these experiences to discuss during interviews. It is therefore important to find ways to demonstrate your competency in these skills. Whenever you are given the opportunity to develop and present a lesson, be sure to save the formal outline of the lesson itself, your reflection on how the lesson turned out, photos of final products such as bulletin boards or student projects, worksheets you have created, and student samples. Be sure to get permission from students' parents to keep copies of work samples in your portfolio. Artifact 6.1 presents Lindsey Ogden's lesson outline, the assessment outcomes, and Lindsey's reflections on the lesson outcome.

Just as there are cooperating teachers from whom you learn the best ideas, sometimes there are also teachers from whom you learn (by negative example) what you surely will *not* do in your own classroom. In the following excerpt from her first professional clinical experience, Liz Newby reflects on the methods and style of her cooperating teacher. By describing what she hopes to try in her own room and praising "Mrs. C.'s" ideas, Liz is also demonstrating her own teaching values.

> After working with Mrs. C., I definitely want to try a word wall. I found this to be extremely helpful when the children are learning "high frequency" words that they find in the books and poems they read. The word wall served as a basis for the words Mrs. C. expected them to read, and eventually, to spell. She also had the students keep "toughies boxes" at their desks. These were words that were giving students trouble and that they needed extra practice with. Whenever there was down-time Mrs. C. would have the students either work on these words or read books from their book boxes. I will always remember how well organized Mrs. C. was. That is something that is important to me. She was also very good at explaining the day's activities to the children so that they knew what was going to happen during the day. She always tried to involve them in the decision-making process. She definitely used a literacy framework. She was always finding what worked best with her students.

On the other hand, notice how Stephanie Brenner tactfully describes her dislikes in terms of her experiences with a cooperating teacher whose style of management differed from her own.

> I do not like . . .
>
> > Being disorganized. I am generally a very organized person, but Mrs. X. was extremely disorganized. It sort of drove me nuts, but I was flexible. It did reinforce how important it is to be organized as a teacher because of all the paperwork I will deal with. Trying to locate papers and books wasted a great deal of time, not to mention it appears very unprofessional. I am sure she also misplaced some of the

From the Real World

Teaching English-Language Learners: 10 Tips
Patience Henkle

1. It is imperative that teachers form positive, caring relationships with their students. This is the key to becoming a successful teacher. Find out about your students' lives; connect with them; tell them about your life. Ask them what they're going to do on the weekend. Tell them stories. Show them pictures of your family. If students feel cared about and feel that you have a genuine interest in who they are, then they will be invested in the learning process. School will become more meaningful to them, and this can only enhance learning.

2. Create a learning atmosphere that is open and tolerant; one that not only recognizes diversity, but celebrates it. Do not establish a punitive environment in which students are prevented from communicating in their native language. Remember that language is closely related to identity. Language learning is a very complicated process; the learning of academic language is even more challenging when hindered by the schools' subtractive devaluing of non-native students' language.

3. Use a "Country of the Month" bulletin board to highlight the countries and cultures of each of your students. Assign a different topic for each student to research (e.g., art, music, history, map and flag, holidays, language, etc.). This is a great way for teachers to tap into the great wealth of diversity and cultural knowledge that students have. It is also a great way to connect students' backgrounds with academic content to make for a more meaningful school experience.

4. Play games! Scrabble, Scattegories, and Vocabulary Bingo are perfect for English-language learning.

5. Be their advocate. Make sure they are getting the kind of support that they need in their mainstream classes so that they don't fall through the cracks. Collaborate with mainstream teachers. Modify tests. Create study guides. Make flash cards. Build background knowledge.

6. Display student work. Don't let there be any white space on your classroom walls. Show off the great work they've done! Also, keep examples of your students' best work. When you assign the project next year, you will have a benchmark to show your students.

7. Keep portfolios. This is a great way to compile data and demonstrate growth. Have students fold a sheet of construction paper in half and decorate the covers. Students should keep their best work in their portfolios, plus all tests, quizzes, and papers. When parents come, you will have something ready to show them.

8. Have high expectations, and do not accept anything less. Students will rise to the occasion if you believe in them. You'll be amazed at how much language a young person can acquire in just a short amount of time. English-language learners need support, but they don't need to be coddled. Because they are acquiring a new language as well as content, they need to work extra hard.

9. Be flexible. You will constantly need to assess and adjust accordingly. Always check for understanding. If they're not getting it, it's your fault! Always be ready to change your lesson plan, if necessary.

10. Be enthusiastic. If you think it's boring, how do you think they feel? Think of new and interesting ways to present material. Break the mold. Surprise them! Be creative, and have fun.

6.1   Artifact

In the following lesson written and implemented by Lindsey Ogden during her first professional clinical experience, notice how Lindsey follows the above recommendations—she includes the lesson outline, assessment outcomes, and her reflection on the lesson outcome.

Lesson Outline

I. Type of Lesson—Reading Comprehension Lesson

II. Class Information—Fifth Grade
    A. Reading levels ranging from second to sixth grade.
    B. Diversity—9 girls, 11 boys, all native English speakers; 3 African American students; 1 Asian American student; several students with low SES; several students pulled out for extra help with the special education teacher; and 1 student receiving speech instruction.

III. Background Knowledge
    A. Students must be able to sit quietly while listening to a story read aloud.
    B. Students must be able to summarize events into paragraph format.

IV. Rationale

In this lesson, students will become more familiar with summarizing story content while creating a visual to represent their summary.

V. Objectives and Assessment Plans
    A. Standard A. Listen attentively by facing the speaker, making eye contact, and paraphrasing what is said. (4.A.1a)
        i. Objective #1—The students will face the teacher most of time, making eye contact some of the time.
        ii. Assessment Plan for Objective #1—The teacher will observe the students and make a mental note of those students who are not making eye contact or are not facing the reader most of the time. When the lesson is finished, the teacher will record this data for future reference.
    B. Standard B. Summarize and make generalizations from content and relate to purpose of material. (1.C.2d)
        i. Objective #2—Students will complete their section of the group pentarama to represent the summary of a chapter from the book.

        ii. Assessment Plan for Objective #2—The teacher will collect the pentaramas after the presentation and check them for completion. The students will have written a short paragraph to summarize their chapter and will have drawn an illustration to accompany to the summary.

VI. Materials
    A. *A Colonial Sea Captain* by J. L. Branse, published by PowerKids Press on August 1, 2002.
    B. *A Day in the Life of a Colonial Soldier* by J. L. Branse and Jennifer Landau, published by PowerKids Press on August 1, 2002.
    C. Supplies: One blank sheet of paper per student, scissors, paste/tape/glue stick/staples, pen/pencil, and markers/colored pencils/crayons.

VII. Grouping Techniques

The students first will be placed into groups of 10. One group will read about the sea captain and the other will read about the soldier. Then both groups will be split in half so that there are five children per group. Within the groups of five, the students will break up the chapters chunked by the teacher and summarize them using the pentarama design. These groups will be based on the ability to work well together as this project will take collaboration. Students with lower abilities will be intermixed with students with higher abilities. It is possible that the students with higher abilities students will aid the students with lower abilities.

VIII. Procedures
    A. Introduction

Begin the lesson by breaking the classroom into two groups, preferably two groups of 10.

Next, explain to the class that they will be creating a pentarama to summarize a story about a person from colonial times. Explain that the two groups will be reading different stories so each group will have to do a good job summarizing through a short oral presentation.

Then explain to the students that this lesson goes along with their social studies unit on colonial times and that this will help them get a firmer grasp on summarizing.

    B. Lesson Steps
        i. Students will be broken into two groups. These groups will be chosen by the teacher to ensure that the students will work well together.

ii. Each group will be taken to a separate area so that a teacher or aide may read them the story.

iii. After completing the story, the students will view a demonstration on how to create their piece of the pentarama.

iv. Now the groups will be split in half again so that there are about five students per group. These groups should work together to create a pentarama that summarizes their half of the book.

v. If needed (especially if this is their first time with a pentarama) the teacher will demonstrate the process again while they follow along, creating their own.

vi. Now that they have cut their paper and understand how it will look when completed, each child should write down a summary of his or her portion of the story and include an interesting illustration to accompany that summary.

vii. When each student is completed with his or her piece, it will be placed into the final pentarama design (these will be five-sided figures).

viii. The students will then gather back in their classroom and be seated.

ix. If children have completed the activity in a satisfactory manner, teacher will make positive comments. If time and space are available, hang the pentaramas around the room.

Sample Questions

1. What happened to the whale population after many years of hunting? Why?
2. What did a typical colonial solider wear?
3. Do you think it would have been hard to live in colonial times? Why or why not?

C. Closure

Now that the students have come back together, they will listen to the summaries of all of the groups so that they may learn about the other story without actually reading it. Each student will read his or her summary and explain the illustration they drew to go along with it. After each student has had a turn to summarize orally, ask if there are any questions. If time allows ask some general comprehension questions about the books to judge the effectiveness of the lesson. Then tell the class they did wonderfully.

Assessment Outcomes

The students did well during this lesson, though I believe things could have gone smoother. Of the 10 students in my group, 8 were almost constantly making eye contact and showing me that they were listening to the story. Two of the students had to be asked to quiet down or to stop a behavior several times throughout the reading. These students did not reach my first objective. They were rude and disruptive during the reading and were consequently confused when it came to actually creating the project. This took extra time away from the rest of the students and it wore away at their patience.

All of the students met my second objective. Each student in my group of 10 completed their piece of the pentarama. However, some of the pieces were more detailed and thoughtful. On a grading scale, their work would range from mostly A work to some C work. The lower grades were reserved for those who did not follow the directions thoroughly.

Reflection

The pentaramas turned out great and proved to be an excellent way to get the children to summarize parts of a story for their classmates. The best part of this project was when the students went back to the classroom and shared their summaries and pictures with the rest of the class. I believe this went well because children enjoy sharing their work. They also liked sharing a new story with the half of the class that did not read the same story. The illustrating was, of course, their favorite part of the project, but they also enjoyed the way the pieces fit together to make one object when they were finished.

The biggest problem during this activity was two students' behaviors. These students were talking and moving about while I was reading the story. I had to stop the story to move them to different seats, away from each other. Then I had to stop the story again because one child was throwing markers at the other child. Finally, the well-behaved students had enough of their horseplay and disrespect, so they began to yell at the misbehaving students. Therefore, during this time I had to curb the misbehavior of the two students while assuring the other students I was handling the situation and did not need their help. Eventually, I did get all of the students' attention. I continued with the story and

Continued

6.1   Artifact   *Continued*

then only one student was being disruptive. I moved closer to him and he seemed to lessen his misbehavior. When my classroom teacher came to check on me, she saw that the students were fed up with this certain misbehaving child and so she asked him to remove himself from the class and go with her. This student is often removed from group work and even class work because he misbehaves at an astonishing rate. I found it frustrating because I had tried several things to get him involved in the story but none of it seemed to make a difference. My classroom teacher assured me that he was having an off day and that there was no working with this behavior in a group setting.

To curb misbehavior, next time I will create a seating arrangement for the groups and be sure that all of the art supplies are out of reach until they are needed. I will also be sure to explain the importance of listening to the story and following directions to show what I expect from the students before I begin the lesson. I think that doing this will create a better learning environment. The students will feel more comfortable if they have a better understanding of what is expected of them.

Having the children work in groups makes me think more and more about how and why to group them. In this lesson, my classroom teacher formed the groups herself to ensure the students worked well together. Though I believe this strategy would be useful in some instances, it seemed to fail for this lesson. In addition, students need to be told what is expected and then held accountable for their actions.

Again, with this lesson I have learned that patience is key. Though it was frustrating to deal with the misbehaving student, especially when nothing I was doing to intervene was helping, I kept my cool. I think that being patient is one of the most important things a teacher can do. If the teacher loses his or her patience, there is no hope of keeping the student involved and controlled. With patience, a teacher shows that he or she is an adult and students may respect the teacher as an authority figure. I think it is also important that a misbehaving student does not see you lose your patience to a major degree because this will show what he or she is doing is ineffective. I hope that this will keep the misbehavior from becoming extreme.

students' homework. She figured they did not turn it in and so they would have to redo it. Many times the students became understandably frustrated with her.

- Cramming too many activities into too short of a time period. I think it would be more beneficial to the students (as well as the whole feeling of the classroom) to spend more focused, meaningful time on each activity rather than try to do all activities every day and rush through them.

- Stretching out writing essays. I think it would be better to write an entire essay in one or two days. In my clinical classroom they took an entire week to write an essay. The first day would be brainstorming. The second and third days were interchanged because Mrs. X. was experimenting. One day would be for the introduction and the other day would be for the body. The fourth day was dedicated to the conclusion and the fifth involved editing and writing the formal copy to hand in. I felt like this was too broken up. The second day the students would have to brainstorm again to remember what they were writing about and by the end of the week they were very confused about which paragraphs went where. They got to the point where they did not even know what they were writing about.

Liz and Stephanie both express their values and teaching styles through their reflections on how others teach, motivate, and organize their students. What have you seen or learned from others that you might include in your portfolio section on planning?

✄ Curricular Modifications for Diverse Learners

More and more, students with mild, moderate, or severe learning or behavioral disabilities are receiving their instruction in an age-appropriate regular education environment. *Inclusion* and *regular education initiative (REI)* are two terms for such an instructional delivery model. Inclusion and REI students are believed by their teachers and parents to benefit socially and academically from being around peers who have not been identified as disabled.

The following thoughts are Ginger Law's, a classroom aide in a self-contained classroom for middle school students with behavior disorders. Ginger is in the dual position of having the opportunity to use her parenting skills in the classroom and her teaching skills in her home. As an aide working with students with behavior disorders and learning disabilities, Ginger must be able to implement modifications. As a parent of a student with learning disabilities, Ginger must also know what modifications to ask for and to expect. The implications of Ginger's thoughts are paramount to you.

> As a teacher's assistant in a classroom for students with behavior disorders, I use many modifications. Most of the students have learning disabilities as well as behavior problems. Dictation is used to help the students with power writing. When they are given the opportunity to think aloud without worrying about getting the ideas on paper, it gives them a boost in their thinking process. At times, the work is lessened. Or, with multiple choice question tests or worksheets, the number of choices are cut down. Another important modification is allowing students extended time to turn in their work. Some students do below-grade-level work. If the student has visual problems, large-type print books are used; and if none are available, then enlarged copies of text are made. The most often used modification is to either read to the student or use audio tapes.
>
> My experiences in this position have taught me to help my own child with learning disabilities. I know what modifications to his IEP will ensure his success in the classroom. The modifications he has access to are audio and/or videotapes, having tests read to him, being allowed to dictate responses, and having extended time.
>
> I expect the teachers who work with my child to know, and implement, the modifications that my child can use. As a teacher's assistant, I believe that you should use whatever modifications are needed to prevent stress (for both the student and the teacher) and to promote self-esteem. But most important, I believe that parent–teacher contact is vital to the success of both the student and the teacher.

Whether you are getting your degree in regular education or special education, you must be aware of the need for modifications and also be skilled at both creating and implementing them. Parents like Ginger may be included as part of the interview team. Additionally, administrators always look for teachers who are willing to use a variety of methods to teach and to assess students with diverse learning needs. Remember, the willingness to modify instruction and assessment is also a proactive classroom management technique. What are some modifications you have observed, or perhaps that you have wished you or someone could implement?

One important facet of being an educator is striving to create meaningful lessons that are accessible to students of different abilities and varying backgrounds. In the best-case scenarios, you will have an expert in the field of special education to help you to ensure this worthy goal. Unfortunately, money and space sometimes preclude the possibility of assigning two certified instructors to one group of students. In these cases, you may or may not have an aide or paraprofessional at your disposal, and the certified special educator may be able to make only scheduled appearances. Therefore, whenever you write lesson plans, it is wise to include your ideas for curricular modifications. Whether or not a student is legally labeled as having a learning need with an **Individual Education Plan (IEP),** there will always be students who may benefit either from receiving alternate forms of instruction or from being allowed alternate ways of showing comprehension.

Friend and Bursuck (2002) offer some suggestions for those times when you are at a loss for ideas and do not know where to turn. They suggest joining a professional organization such as the Council for Exceptional Children (CEC), forming a teacher support group, or checking out the supplemental, modifying materials at your local teacher supply store.

✤ Curricular Modification Artifacts

If you create your own list of possible modifications (see Artifacts 6.2 and 6.3), you may wish to also include samples of the curriculum before and after the modifications have been made. Another idea is to divide your modifications list into learning modalities or into forms of presentation. If you use a learning modalities approach, use headings such as:

- Auditory
- Visual
- Kinesthetic
- Tactile

For a list of presentation and performance demand modifications, consider using headings such as:

- Lecture
- Seating
- Printed materials
- Auditory aids
- Visual aids
- Note-taking
- Overhead projector
- Computer presentation
- Lighting
- Chalkboard/white board
- Peer study buddy
- Calculator
- Word processor
- Translation/interpreting

6.2   Artifact

The following list of possible modifications was brainstormed by a group of students in a developmental reading course. If you include previously published lists of modifications in your portfolio, be sure to cite your references.

MODIFICATIONS FOR SPECIAL NEEDS

preferential seating
dictation
oral tests & assignments
technology
calculators
word processors
choices
multiple choice spelling tests
literature response journals
alternate forms of work
talk directly to students with hearing impairments
work in pairs or groups
manipulatives

extra time
hands-on activities
mixed groups
change materials to fit goals
offer challenges at all levels
variety of assessment tools
pretests
role-plays
overheads & other visual aids
reduce size of task
larger print
students tape record answers
books printed in Braille

6.3   Artifact

Eric Spooner is an educator of elementary students with moderate mental retardation. The lesson shown below exemplifies Eric's organizational skills, his insights into the needs of the individual students in his caseload, and his understanding of how to utilize Gardner's multiple intelligences to foster optimum student engagement and growth.

Handwriting Monday
Handwriting Without Tears

Desired Result: Correctly formed letters to ensure lifelong writing proficiency

Benchmark: KG-LA: I. 1.1, 1.3, 2.1–2; 1st—LA: 2.3, 3.1.a–e; 2nd —LA: II. 1.1–2, 3.1–3; 3rd—LA: II. 1.1, 3.3–4; 4th—LA: II. 1.1, 1.6; OAAP: LA (2); SR (Shake Hands with Me)

Gardner's Multiple Intelligences & Bloom's Taxonomy: BK, VL, VS, MR, B1, B2, B3

Resources: Purple book, *Pre-K Teacher's Guide,* which goes with the lime-green workbook, *Get Set for School;* green book, *Handwriting Without Tears Teacher's Guide,* which goes with the orange workbook, *Letters and Numbers for Me;* pink book, *Printing Teacher's Guide,* which goes with the yellow workbook, *My Printing Book;* stickers; HWT Wood Pieces Set; HWT Capital Letter Cards for Wood Pieces; HWT Mat for wood pieces; HWT Slate Chalk Board; small sponge pieces; small chalk pieces; rags.

Effective Instruction: Follow the instructions for teaching the lessons. The page numbers for the lessons and the book are listed in the chart below. Observe each student writing his or her letter to make sure he or she has the mechanics right.

Instructional Strategies: M1, M3, M4

Assessment: Worksheets are assessed according to the standards under the subheading, *Evaluation,* for each lesson in *Pre-K Teacher's Guide, Handwriting Without Tears Teacher's Guide,* and *Printing Teacher's Guide.*

Prompt Hierarchy: Restrictiveness: NE—Natural/Environmental, IV—Indirect Verbal, DV—Direct Verbal, V—Visual, P—Proximity, G—Gesture, PP—Partial Physical, FP—Full Physical; Intensity: M—Minimal, F—Frequent, I—Intense.

Lesson	Wet-Dry-Try	Prompt	Posture	Prompt	Crayon Grip	Prompt	Workbook	Prompt	Notes & Pins
Rachel									
Jamil									
Nathan									
Ellen									
Joaquim									
Lesson	*Pre-K Teacher's Guide*								
Workbook Page	*Get Set for School*								

Materials:

Codes:

Gardner's Multiple Intelligences: BK—Bodily/Kinesthetic, LM—Logical/Mathematical, VL—Verbal/Linguistic, VS—Visual/Spatial, IE—Interpersonal, IA—Intrapersonal, MR—Musical/Rhythmic, N—Naturalist, EX—Existential.

Instructional Strategies: M1—Identify similarities & differences; M2—Summarizing & note taking; M3—Reinforcing effort & providing recognition; M4—Providing homework & practice; M5—Using both linguistic & nonlinguistic representations; M6—Incorporating cooperative learning; M7—Setting objectives & providing feedback; M8—Generating & testing hypothesis; M9—Using cues, questions, and advance organizers.

FIGURE 6.1

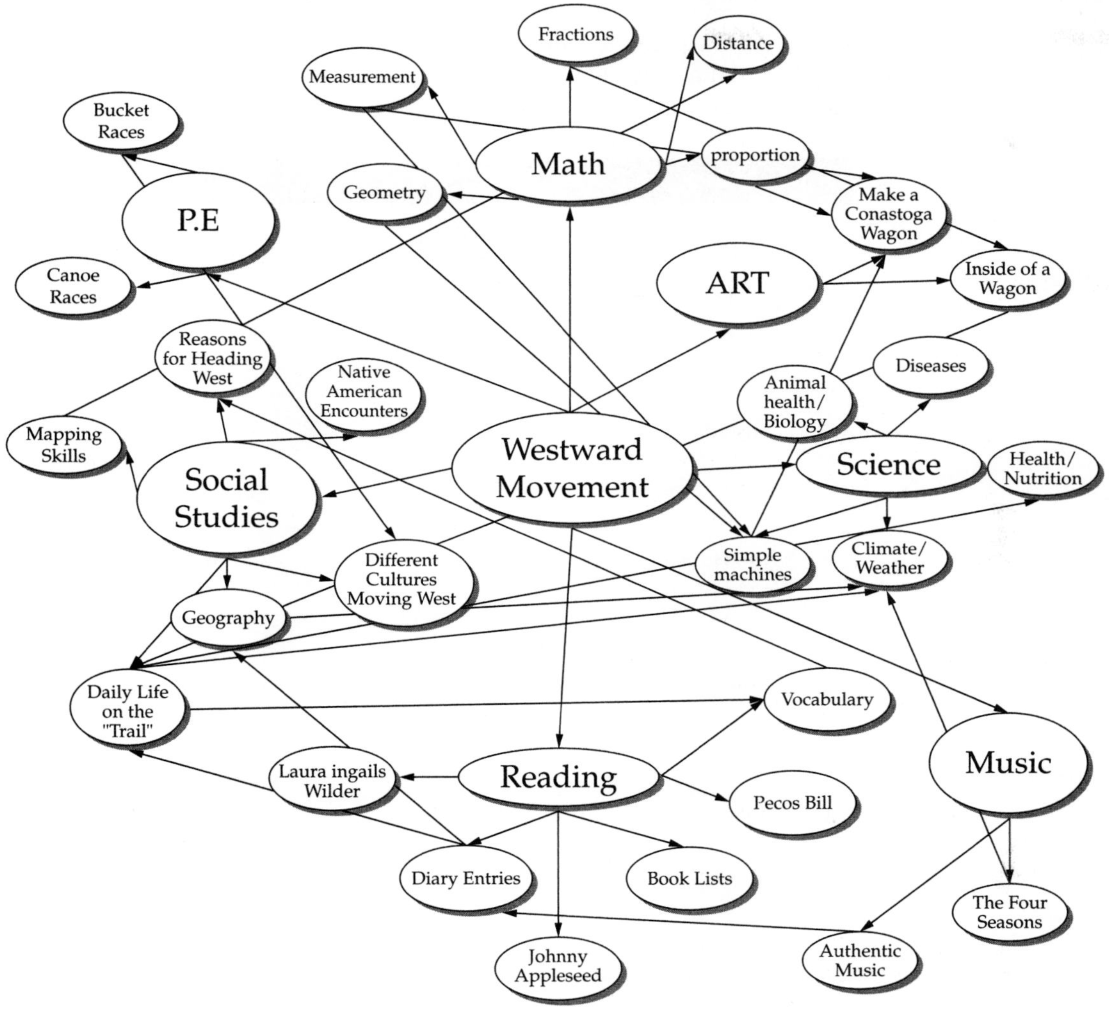

Differentiated Instruction

Whether you are a third-grade classroom teacher, a middle school art teacher, a high school science teacher, or an elementary physical education teacher, you will be expected to adapt your curriculum to meet the needs of the diverse learners in your classes. Another method for meeting diverse learning needs is differentiated instruction. Sometimes known as multilevel instruction, differentiated instruction is a technique that may use different modalities of learning, different difficulty levels of learning, or a combination of these strategies to teach the diverse learners within one classroom.

In Figures 6.1 and 6.2, Danielle Cournaya and her teammates in a middle school methods course present their vision for, and assessment of, an interdisciplinary unit. What personal characteristics are displayed in such an example of teamwork?

⚒ Considerations

School administrators look for competent, caring, and insightful teachers who create lesson plans to engage all types of students in their classes. How will you show that your lessons reflect well-thought-out strategies and encompass the principles of a particular model of teaching?

FIGURE 6.2

Rubric for Final Group Project

		Provides details written or graphically represented about western movement learned through participation in this unit.	Enthusiasm and participation of group members is evident in the creation and presentation of their project.
4	Exceeds	Includes 18–20 details.	All group members share equally in the creation and presentation of the project with evident enthusiasm.
3	Meets	Includes 13–17 details.	Group members all participate in creation and presentation of project with evident enthusiasm.
2	Below	Includes 8–12 details.	Group members participate in creation and presentation of project with limited enthusiasm.
1	Does Not Meet	Includes 0–7 details.	Project creation and presentation is unevenly shared by group with limited enthusiasm of most group members.

Reference

Friend, M., & Bursuck, W. (2002). *Including students with special needs*. Boston: Allyn & Bacon.

Suggested Resources

Online Articles

Kern, L., Delaney, B., Clarke, S., Dunlap, G., & Childs, K. (2001, Winter). Improving the classroom behavior of students with emotional and behavioral disorders using individualized curricular modifications. *Journal of Emotional and Behavioral Disorders*. Retrieved from http://drmts.com/edu496/schedule/article.htm

Williams, J. (2001, June). Adaptations & accommodations for students with disabilities. Resource List 15 (BIB 15). Retrieved from http://nichcy.org/pubs/bibliog./bib15txt.htm

Print

Tomlinson, C. A. (2001). *How to differentiate in mixed-ability classrooms.* Alexandria, VA: Association for Supervision and Curriculum Development.

Web Sites

To find more articles on lesson plans, differentiated instruction, or curricular modifications, go to:

http://www.findarticles.com

Teaching Mathematics to Gifted Students in a Mixed-Ability Classroom Web page:

http://www.kidsource.com/education/teach.gift.math.html

PE Central.org's goal is to provide the latest information about developmentally appropriate physical education programs for children and youth. Go to:

http://www.pecentral.org/index.html

Reflecting on Your Preprofessional Experiences

> Reflection in teaching is a process that takes place over long periods of time in which connections, long strands of connections, are made between one's values, purposes, and actions towards engaging students successfully in their own meaningful language.
>
> *(Lyons, 1998)*

Good teachers are insightful. They combine their desire to share their knowledge with their daunting goal of meeting the individual needs of each student. One great contributor to the development of insight is the practice of reflection, or **reflective teaching.** In your portfolio, reflective artifacts will demonstrate to your future employers, peer review teams, or national standard review boards that you make intentional decisions. You are a teacher who monitors and adjusts your instruction to meet the needs of your students. Because you regularly reflect upon your lessons, your communication skills, and your curricular knowledge, you are obviously a teacher whose goal is to use your ongoing, lifelong learning to benefit your students, your school, and even your community at large.

INTASC: Standard 8—Assessment

Assessment does not apply only to student work and grades. Within this section of your portfolio, include a reflection on a lesson or unit that you taught. By including reflection within the assessment portion of your portfolio, you are acknowledging that teachers must also assess their own competencies and are responsible for the successes and failures of their students.

TWS: Reflection and Self-Evaluation

Within the Teacher Work Sample Portfolio, it is suggested that you include a short reflection of your teaching methods and performance to observed student learning outcomes. This should be a 2–3 page reflection on a unit that you have taught. It may include a variety of student products, and should demonstrate your effective or developing teaching strategies. This section should have its own folder, link, or tab depending upon your portfolio style.

✄ Goals of Reflection

Reflective thinking is a means to enhance self-awareness, create a positive (albeit sometimes uncomfortable) lack of complacency, and keep oneself focused on improving professional practices. Also known as *reflective teaching*, reflective thinking exercises are tools for growth. When you practice reflection, you may be surprised to note that you are achieving several goals at the same time.

- One goal of reflection is self-evaluation. Ask yourself, "How do I feel about how my lesson turned out today?" Or ask, "Am I happy with myself as a teacher? If so, what growth am I observing? What new successes? If I'm dissatisfied, in what specific areas can I improve? What is in my control, and what is not?"
- Another goal of reflection considers your impact on your students. When considering your students, focus on questions of comprehension, learning climate, frustration levels, and mastery of skills. "Whom did I observe showing mastery of the concept? Who was unusually quiet? Why did Billy act out today during the lesson, when he has not been a problem before? How can I get more students to volunteer answers? What's the best way to get Mary to try some problems on her own before she asks for help?"
- A third goal of reflective thinking is to make connections. These connections may relate to ideas of instruction, commonalties across curriculum, inspirations for interdisciplinary units, or even connections between causes and effects that occur in your classroom environment or between you and your colleagues, you and your students, or you and your students' parents.

From the Real World

Lori Delk

I spend my days in a colorful, cheerful, and vibrant environment. Walls are covered with positive statements; they display clear instructions, steps in a process, or positive words offering encouragement that promotes students to question. There are items from all over the world displayed, some on posters, and some in three dimensions. . . . A giant guardian serpent watches over the room where small tables are arranged in clusters of five. Taped to the corner of each small table is an affirmation reminding its reader that each day belongs to her or him; it is their day to seize. Those who pass through those doors are respected and valued for the individuals they are. In addition, they are expected to be responsible; they are responsible to themselves and to others. I have entered the world of 4B at Frank Hall Elementary School, Mr. Britton's fourth-grade class of 2003. Mr. Britton created an atmosphere full of life. . . .

Respect begins with the morning greeting of each student. The daily affirmation reminds the students that they are in control of their future. Positive statements throughout the room continue to remind students that they are the only ones who will choose their destiny. Step-by-step processes are available to remind the students the academic process they will need to achieve success. My goal as a future teacher is to empower students. I will do this in part, by applying what I have learned through my experience at Frank Hall Elementary School.

- Finally, reflection is involved in your decisions regarding the artifacts that you include in your professional portfolio. Later in this chapter we'll explore several questions to reflect upon as you develop your portfolio.

✵ Models of Reflection

From your first preprofessional experience to your application for a national master teaching certificate, you will have many reasons to reflect. The best way to keep records of your reflections is to maintain a reflection journal. In your journal, you may wish to follow Schon's (1995) guidelines for reflection. Schon suggests that there are two major types of reflective thinking, *reflection-on-action*, and *reflection-in-action*. Reflection-on-action relates to the time you take after completing an action (whether an interaction, lesson, or assignment). Reflection-in-action involves thinking about what you are doing *while* you are doing it. Killion and Todnem (1991) suggest that there is a third type of reflection known as *reflection-for-action* which, naturally, addresses planning for future actions.

✵ Examples of Reflection

The following are excerpts from students' reflections. Two of these students are in their first preprofessional courses, and the other is a student teacher. As you read these selections, refer back to the goals of reflection and the models of reflection noted in this chapter. In our first example from

Katie Levernier, she shares both her excitement and her fears about her first clinical. Additionally, she includes some philosophical goals that she is developing.

> My clinical experience in Middlebrook proved invaluable. I learned a great deal from my cooperating teacher and fellow staff members, but it was my students who taught me most of all. I learned classroom management, positive reinforcements, and effective motivations. I also learned about each child academically and socially. I didn't know exactly what to expect entering this clinical. Would the teacher consider me an inconvenience or would she appreciate my input and strive to help me learn? Should I sit and wait to be asked to help, or should I dive right in without being asked? These and many other questions were on my mind as I drove to Middlebrook on my very first day as a teacher. I was excited and nervous, giddy and extremely tired. From the moment I entered the classroom, Miss Sibrovski, my cooperating teacher, made me feel extremely welcome to ask questions, get involved with the students and their work, and even offer ideas and suggestions. I walked around answering all kinds of questions, tested the children individually in math and reading, and walked them to gym class. I knew immediately that I had chosen the right path for my life.
>
> . . . My classroom is going to be a positive learning environment where children grow both academically and socially. I want to have an open and loving rapport with my students. I feel that to be a great teacher you must understand where your students are coming from and what kinds of situations they may be dealing with at home. For example, if a student's parents are getting divorced this will definitely take a toll on his school work, his temper control, and even his motivation levels. As a teacher, I want to be aware of any conditions in or out of school that may impact my students' learning.

In this next reflection, Stephanie Brenner discusses her students' cultural and socioeconomic backgrounds, and offers some explanation of the history of the school's language arts curriculum.

> My first clinical experience was in a fifth-grade class in Westchester's Sandburg Elementary School. The class consists of 30 students. There are 16 girls and 14 boys, all 10 to 11 years old. Most are from lower- to lower-middle-class SES. The breakdown of ethnicities is as follows: 11 Mexican American students, 12 African Americans, 6 Caucasians, and 1 Asian American. This was my first experience in a classroom where the white children represent the minority.
>
> Before I discuss my cooperating teacher's framework, I should give some information about the recent history of the school's reading philosophy. This is the first year my teacher, Mrs. Lauriat, taught fifth grade. The previous 11 years she taught third-grade classes at Sandburg. Three years ago, the school took away the teachers' basal, shifting to the whole language approach to reading. The teachers had to come up with their own resources, ordering books from Scholastic and making lots of Xeroxes for worksheets from extension activity books. After some time, the teachers realized the students were just not learning how to read. Test scores proved it.
>
> . . . I want to try to . . .

- Incorporate more language arts into social studies and science. More thematic units would allow for a smoother flow throughout the day.
- Have several reward systems that are meaningful to the students. I know this creates extrinsic motivation, but at least there would be some motivation. For example, I would have a chart for spelling. For every

A, a child gets a star. If the entire class earns 300 stars before Christmas, then they can have a pizza party or something else they choose as a class.

- Encourage students to write well by having them write for an audience (besides me). I would have the class create a newspaper biweekly. Each child would be assigned some sort of writing responsibility (maybe switch off who writes the front page story), and the newspapers would be copied for the class and their parents to read.

The following reflection was written during Lisa Owens's student teaching experience. As you can see, she learned as much from what went wrong as she did from what went smoothly. It is important to demonstrate the ability to learn from one's mistakes.

> This week I faced two struggles with teaching, planning, and classroom management. With planning I realized that there is a lot that goes into a week, and figuring out a logical sequence and creative ways of presenting the information isn't always easy. This was my first week teaching reading, and although the book is full of things to do, I found myself confused. At times it seemed like there were so many things to do that I wondered if I were going to be able to get through them all. And other times I felt that the activities given were repetitive or not enough and I didn't know where to go. I guess this is why this is my time to learn. I feel that the first week of teaching a new subject is the hardest because the subject is unfamiliar. Something that gives me hope is to remember how I felt at the start of teaching different subjects. For example, I felt the same way about science at first, but by the end of the unit I saw definite improvement in my lesson presentation and how well the lesson went overall. After planning and teaching reading for one week, I feel that I am more aware of what it entails and hope that the next week will come easier. I'm sure I will still need input as to the format and order of teaching all the areas at first, but I hope to grow in my abilities and see improvement.
>
> Second, I struggled with classroom management. The students are a talkative group but limits still need to be kept. On Wednesday they were so loud during reading groups! I am hoping the plan of timing their transitions will help to calm them down and make them view me as someone they need to listen too. The students don't view me as a real teacher and this makes gaining their respect and willingness to listen harder. Knowing this, as my time in front of the class increases, I need to make sure I am being firm with them so they do know I mean business. However, I do hope to keep their wonderful energy for learning, as well as the fun classroom environment they love so much.

✄ Artifact Rationales

As we addressed in Chapter 2, it is vital that you are able to articulate the value of the artifacts you include in your portfolio. Good teachers have the ability and the tendency to reflect upon their decisions as well as on the impact of their decisions. Likewise, the artifacts you choose to include in your professional portfolio require reflection. How does a certain artifact convey your skills? What will the future employer learn about you by viewing the artifact? What did you learn from the experience represented by the artifact? And finally, how does inclusion of this artifact demonstrate your achievement of professional teaching standards?

✗ Considerations

Reflection-on-action, reflection-in-action, and reflection-for-action are all important when conveying how your experiences have affected you. Reflection-on-action occurs after an experience; reflection-in-action occurs while you are participating in the new experience; and reflection-for-action occurs when you plan how to improve next time. Following this three-pronged approach will guide you to a meaningful evolution of your teaching and of your students' learning.

References

Killion, J. P., & Todnem, G. R. (1991). A process for personal theory building. *Educational Leadership, 48*(6), 14–16.

Lyons, N. (1998). Reflection in teaching: Can it be developmental? A portfolio perspective. *Teacher Education Quarterly, 25*(1), 115–127.

Schon, D. A. (1995). *A reflective practitioner*. New York: Ashgate.

Suggested Resources

Print

Arends, R. I. (2004). *Learning to teach*. Boston: McGraw-Hill.

Arends, R. I., Winitzky, N. E., & Tannenbaum, M. D. (2001). *Exploring teaching.* Boston: McGraw-Hill.

Borko, H., Michalec, P., Timmons, M., & Siddle, J. (1997). Student teaching portfolios: A tool for promoting reflective practice. *Journal of Teacher Education, 48*(5), 345–357.

Costantino, P. M., & De Lorenzo, M. N. (2006). *Developing a professional teaching portfolio: A guide for success*. College Park: University of Maryland.

Farris, P. J. (1999). *Teaching, bearing the torch*, 2nd ed. Boston: McGraw-Hill.

Sadker, M., & Sadker, D. (2000). *Teachers, schools, & society*, 5th ed. Boston: McGraw-Hill.

Web Sites

Reflective Action Web site:

http://www.reflectiveaction.com/ramodel.html

NEA: Become a Reflective Teacher Web page:

http://www.nea.org/teachexperience/tresk030605.html

Preparing for Interviews

✻ Using Your Portfolio in Interviews

In galleries and art shows you'll find many artists who save copies of their work in portfolios to document and show to future customers. In schools we use portfolios to qualitatively, holistically assess the progress of our K–12 students. In the business world, stock portfolios give a clear picture of someone's investments. The word *portfolio* is used in many ways; however, the idea of providing a clear picture remains a consistent portion of portfolio use across disciplines. As educators you will use your portfolios in myriad ways. In this chapter we will discuss how to utilize your teaching portfolio in your quest for employment.

✻ Choosing Your Interview Portfolio

Comprehensive versus Abbreviated Portfolios

A common misconception about creating portfolios is that they are not worth using during interviews because principals do not have time to look through such unwieldy packets of information. It is true that if you attempted to give each potential employer your **comprehensive** (unabridged) **portfolio,** you would likely be spending an inordinate amount of time and money on an ill-advised endeavor. (Imagine an administrator sitting at a desk with 200 applications for a position, and each applicant has sent a copy of his or her comprehensive portfolio.) The fact that comprehensive portfolios may be inappropriate to submit for interviews does not, however, mean that the idea of using portfolios at all during interviews is also ill-advised. In reality, well-organized, abbreviated portfolios can readily demonstrate your skills in the context of what you have researched about the district with whom you are interviewing.

Traditional versus Electronic Portfolios

As described earlier, when we use the term *traditional* to describe a portfolio, we are referring to the actual paper, hard copies of your artifacts. These portfolios tend to be stored in page protectors and large binders, or in accordion files. Now that it has become easier to scan documents or photograph them with digital cameras, there are alternatives to the traditional format. We refer to these alternatives as electronic portfolios. The two main types of electronic portfolios are digital portfolios and Web portfolios.

Digital Portfolios

As we noted in Chapter 3, digital portfolios may be submitted on disk or CD-ROM, or may be sent by e-mail as attachments. We do not recommend sending e-mail with attachments unless the principal or members of the interview team specifically ask you to do so. With digital portfolios, interviewers may appreciate being able to access your information without having to go online, and may print out the pages they find most relevant to their interests. A possible drawback is if your technology is more sophisticated than that of the interview team. First impressions are important, and if their first impression of you is the frustration of being unable to open your digital portfolio, you start out the interview process on a negative note.

Web-based portfolios are better suited for those who prefer to surf the Internet and are adept at downloading files. Like digital portfolios, Web-based portfolios offer you a multimedia opportunity to shine. With animation, sound, Web links, and video clips, you provide the viewer with a fuller picture of yourself and your abilities. It is vital that you make your Web site user-friendly—ensure simple transitions between links, double-check that any files you have posted open easily on other computers. Ask others to do the same. You might

From the Real World

Principal Michael Devereaux

I feel our district uses an excellent interview practice. We do not interview in isolation. We will compose a team for interviewing. The team will consist of the building principal, another teacher at the same grade level, perhaps a teaching assistant who may work with the person, other principal(s). During the interview the candidates will present a 10-minute lesson of their choice on a given topic (e.g., *"You are a third-grade teacher. Present a 10-minute language arts lesson"*). This is really where an excellent candidate will shine. However, a candidate is not hired on presenting a lesson only. Another important part of the interview is the written part. Interviewers are asked to focus on spelling, grammar, and content—in that order. (Note: ALL interviewers are given an orientation prior to the actual interviews.)

What to never, ever do during an interview: DO NOT display extremes. DO be humorous, but not obnoxious. DO explain yourself, but not too lengthily. DO be calm, but not sloppy. DO be professional, but not aloof. Again, DO NOT DISPLAY EXTREMES.

Things I look for in a beginning teacher are those qualities listed above. I also focus on and ask about being a team player, a collaborative teacher, and above all someone who is kind and caring to children. It is called the "art" of teaching.

There are three types of questions that I ask during an interview: informational, situational, and philosophical. The situational questions can be very interesting and revealing about a candidate.

The main advice I give to those who ask me is to be yourself. Get hired because of what and who you are. If you are a kind, caring person, then display that. If you are a grumpy, short-tempered individual, then become something other than a teacher.

even ask friends with older versions of Windows or Macintosh to try your digital or Web-based portfolio to see if they can open it.

✧ Providing Brochures

Some teaching candidates choose to provide their potential employers with brief brochures. The **brochure** offers the basic personal information—name, address, degree program, and so on, and also offers the address of the candidate's Web site. Each page within the Web site may be listed and summarized in the brochure. Figure 8.1 shows Carla Raynor's brochure. Notice that she has organized the brochure with INTASC standards, and then personalized each of the standards by listing the artifacts that demonstrate her experiences.

✧ Choosing Artifacts Based on School District Information

Once you have learned the basic information about a job opening, you can research the district or school and choose the artifacts that will show your experiences and interests relevant to that specific opening. If it is a diversely populated area, you will be sure to include your artifacts pertaining to your

FIGURE 8.1

Portfolio Overview

To furnish the means of acquiring knowledge is...the greatest benefit that can be conferred upon mankind.

John Quincy Adams
Carla Raynor
511 South Ninth Avenue
Rorydon, Illinois 88756

Communication

Increasing Language Arts Capabilities

Enhancement Words
- Employed both verbal and visual instruction
- Designed graphic representations to help students understand concept of detail
- Encouraged student participation with magnetic words on board to build sentence detail

Using Variety of Communication

Pick-a-Pizza Story Pie
- Provided students with a choice of novels and projects in a creative environmnetnt

Assessment

Designing Unit Assessments

Shackleton and the Endurance
- Wrote overview of six day assessment plan including formal and informal assessments
- Used technology to create rubrics and tests
- Generated rubrics for assessment and self-evaluation throughout unit

Creating Informal Assessments

Weather, Sky and Seasons Unit
- Composed original worksheet combining weather and temperature ideas from basal
- Developed science log for informal assessment

Content Knowledge

Teaching Social Studies

Unit of Study on China
- Taught concepts including language, customs, food, tangrams, and celbrations
- Used various children's fiction and non-fiction trade books for reading and reference source
- Provided each student with a China folder filled with unit projects and photograph of culminating activity of eating a Chinese meal

Adapting Dental Unit

Mini-unit on Dental Health
- Created brushing calendar, toothbrushes, tooth booklets, and read trade books on dental care
- Used science experiment to simulate tooth decay

Human Development & Learning

Enhancing Language Arts and Writing

Family Holiday Stories
- Used children's literature as stepping stone to writing process
- Introduced storytelling with descriptive words and details
- Provided whole class and one-on-one support throughout the writing procedure

Developing New Skills

Instructional Lesson on Interviewing Skills
- Modeled interview procedure with mentor teacher
- Designed interviewing hint sheet for students
- Provided structured atmosphere for first-time interviewers

Collaborative Relationships

Communicating with Parents/Students

Letters to Parents and First Grade
- Send home introductory letter to parents during each clinical experience
- Wrote letters to first grade to help establish relationship with students and metor teacher

Reflection & Professional Growth

Practicing Self-Reflections

Teaching Logs
- Wrote reflective logs throughout three clinical experiences and explained growth, standards correlation and improvement for future lessons

Participating in Conferences and Class

IEA/NEA Conferences and Grant Writing
- Participated in conference seminars and online grant writing class to exapande knwonwledge

Professional Conduct

Professional Training

Ethical Seminar and In-Service Training
- Took part in Ethical Fitness for Student Leaders
- Attended Creating and Effective Literacy Program

Faculty Training

Language Arts Rubrics Presentation
- Reflected and applied information on language arts rubrics from KIDS seminar

Diversity

Integrating Multiple Disciplines

Listening Activity
- Designed activity using historical tradebook Pink & Say
- Formulated activity to meet variety of language arts and social studies curriculm requirements
- Created project appropriate for all students at differencet learning levels

Meeting Individual Needs

Language Experience Approach
- Enhanced individual learning through the creation of experience books
- Reflected on project with student's ability in mind

Planning for Instruction

Writing Organized Lesson Plans

Lesson Plan Book
- Wrote weekly plans and included books, page numbers, transparencies, timing and extra items needed for lessons
- Coordinated daily folder system providing all necessary material in one location

Providing Detailed Instruction

Be A Mind Reader
- Planned lesson with the idea that a substitute could easily follow directions
- Provided pacing, questions, and expectations for students

Learning Environment

Reading and Listening Activity

Story Impression
- Involved classroom in discussion to introduce concepts and ideas of You Are Special
- Instructed students on how to combine predictions and questions
- Deepened students' understanding of setting, plot, and characterization

Enhancing Basal Lesson

Tall Tales Project
- Adapted and expanded on basal lesson to include more creativity, writing, and experiences
- Provided opportunity to share and display work

Instructional Delivery

Designing Cooperative Learning Lesson

Holocaust Unit
- Utilized historical fiction tradebook Good Night, Maman as base of lesson
- Encouraged students to work cooperatively as a group with individual jobs
- Generated variety of lesson projects including a bookmark, flyer, comparison poster, map, and Web search

preprofessional and community experiences working with diverse populations. If it is a school that has adopted a specific math or reading series with which you have prior experience, your artifacts documenting this experience will lend an air of expertise. Perhaps this district's middle school is well known for its teaming philosophy. You will be ready for the interview with your interdisciplinary units and your reflections on what you learned at the team meetings. Every school district has issues with classroom management. Whatever you have to say on this topic during the interview will be complemented and supplemented by the artifacts you have chosen to reflect your classroom management philosophy and skills.

✖ Discussing Your Portfolio

Be prepared for anything when you arrive for your interview. Some interviewers will be willing take the time to look through whatever materials you have provided. This is your chance to shine—you will be very impressive if you know your portfolio contents inside and out. Have the artifacts already sorted and labeled for ease of use. When I, Patty Rieman, interviewed for a brand-new position teaching students with behavioral disorders, I came prepared with examples of behavior plans that I had implemented the year before in my previous position. I passed around the plans and explained how they worked. I believe this advance preparation is what convinced the interview team to hire me.

Depending upon the position and the popularity of the school district, there may be hundreds of applicants for the same position. The interview teams for such districts will likely have a set timeline for their interviews and may even have a predetermined structure of which interviewer will ask which question. In this case you may not even have an opportunity to use your portfolio during the interview. If this happens, take the initiative. Thank them for their time, and ask if you may leave the portfolio materials you had prepared for the interview.

✖ Considerations

Your teaching portfolio may be the "deal breaker" in competitive situations. How well you prepare for interviews shows employers your organizational skills, motivation, knowledge of the district, and understanding of the demands of the position. Invest the time in choosing artifacts from your comprehensive portfolio to design an abbreviated portfolio for each interview. Ensure that interviewers can readily access your electronic portfolio. Whenever feasible during the interview, remember to refer to your portfolio artifacts.

Suggested Resources

This site from Winston-Salem State University offers guidelines for interviewing for a teaching position. Go to:

http://www.wssu.edu/student/career/Teachers.htm

This site by Elaine Ernst Schneider and Joanne Mikola asks: "The application has been filled out and submitted, your references are turned in, and now the waiting begins. Will anyone call? And what do you do while you wait? What do you do? You prepare for the next step." Go to:

http://www.lessontutor.com/eesinterview.html

The *Slippery Rock University Teacher Interviewing Guide* includes a terrific list of questions for candidates to ask. Go to:

http://www.sru.edu/print/8256.asp

This site provides links to a job interview guide and job interview tips. Go to:

http://www.job-interview-helper.com/jobinterview/teaching-job-interview-questions/

Southern Illinois University in Edwardsville provides this guide to interviewing for prospective teachers. Go to:

http://www.careers.siue.edu/career/carousel/new/nteacherinterview.htm

Conclusion

By now you've learned what teaching portfolios are, several reasons to create them, and what types of styles are possible. You've read advice from principals and parents. You've seen examples of a wide variety of artifacts, and you should have a good idea of what you plan to include in your own portfolio.

As you create your own portfolio, keep the following suggestions in mind:

- Determine what characteristics about yourself you want your portfolio to convey. Make sure you've included the artifacts that will present you in the best possible light.
- When your portfolio is completed, ask several different people to examine your portfolio and tell you what it conveys about you—are the characteristics you wished to convey coming through?
- For preservice educators, research the school districts you'll be applying to, and arrange your portfolio to meet the goals, standards, and values of those districts.
- If you base your portfolio on a specific set of standards, make that clear—cite the organization responsible for the standards, why you chose them as your focus, and then list the standards themselves.
- Practice presenting your portfolio over and over. Have friends randomly choose a topic, and see how fluently you can turn to the artifacts addressing that topic.
- Have friends tell you whether or not your portfolio is "user-friendly." Is the table of contents helpful? Did you color-code or tab your artifacts? What devices have you included to make your portfolio easy to use?

Thank you for taking the time to use this text. We hope you found it helpful in guiding you through the creation of your portfolio. We also hope that you found the text easy to follow and clear in its purpose of providing a practical approach to building portfolios.

Best wishes,
Patricia L. Rieman and Jeanne Okrasinski

Glossary

Aesthetics—the attractiveness, or the pleasure factor, of a portfolio.

Artifact rationales—the brief descriptions explaining choice of artifacts for inclusion in a portfolio.

Brochure—designed to provide employers with a brief synopsis of such basic personal information as name, address, and degree program; also offers the address of the candidate's Web site.

Career portfolio—serves to keep record of projects, bulletin boards, and units that have been created; in some states, may fulfill requirements for certification renewal.

Classroom management plan—includes expectations of behavior, rules, planned consequences for following (or not following) the rules, and a record-keeping method of monitoring such compliance or lack of compliance.

Collaborative—the ability to work on a team, value others' work, and solicit constructive feedback.

Comprehensive portfolio—an unabridged portfolio; tends to be too large to take to interviews.

Digital portfolio—portfolio that may be submitted on disk or on CD-ROM, or may be sent by e-mail as an attachment.

Efferent—how a teacher expresses information in a portfolio.

Electronic portfolio—"a purposeful collection of work, captured by electronic means, that serves as an exhibit of individual efforts, progress, and achievements in one or more areas" (Wiedmer, 1998).

Essentialism—essentialist teachers tend to believe that the role of schools is to create successful citizens.

Existentialism—influenced by Jean-Paul Sartre and Friedrich Nietzsche, existentialists believe that one must always be free to choose and take responsibility for one's choices.

Experimentalism—experimentalist teachers believe that all subject matter should be connected both to other subjects and to the students' home lives.

Idealism—the oldest known philosophy; idealist teachers tend to believe that all students are capable of being positive, contributing members of society.

Individual Education Plan (IEP)—a legal document providing a team-generated list of modifications, goals, and objectives for students in special education.

Inservice—certified, licensed educator.

Interstate New Teacher Assessment and Support Consortium (INTASC)—a consortium of over 30 states operating under the Council of Chief State School Officials that has developed standards and is now designing an assessment process for initial teacher certification

National Board for Professional Teaching Standards (NBPTS)—this body was created by the Carnegie Forum in the 1990s to recognize outstanding educators.

Perennialism—perennialist teachers tend to see themselves as moral, intellectual authority figures.

Portfolio—an assessment that allows the creator to put his or her best foot forward and document the knowledge and skills mastered through the learning process.

Pragmatism—teachers who are pragmatists tend to be problem solvers who value use of the scientific method.

Preservice—teacher candidates who are undergoing coursework and clinical experiences to become certified, licensed educators.

Progressivism—progressivist teachers believe that students must be prepared to live in an ever-changing society, and thus use such tools as cooperative learning, hands-on activities, and intrinsic rewards.

Reciprocal agreement—states may agree to accept one another's licensure programs; however, the candidate may be required to pass the state's qualifying exams.

Reflection—the ability to think about what one has done in the past so that he or she can apply it to the future; the ability and disposition to think deeply and make decisions about which strategy is appropriate at any given time (Arends et al. 2001).

Reflective teaching—this occurs when connections are made between one's values, purposes, and actions toward engaging students successfully in their own meaningful language.

Social reconstructivism—sometimes referred to simply as *reconstructionism*. Social reconstructionists believe that the function of schools is to teach students to examine social problems and, ultimately, to change society for the better.

Teacher Work Sample (TWS)—exhibits of teaching performance that provide direct evidence of a candidate's ability to design and implement standards-based instruction, assess student learning, and reflect on the teaching and learning process.

Traditional portfolio—a portfolio that is published on paper, not online or on CD-ROM. The traditional portfolio tends to be in a binder or accordion file folder, and its table of contents is organized with tabs.

Web-based portfolio—a portfolio that allows viewers to access the information at their leisure whenever they go online.

Table of Artifacts

Dear Parent/Guardian,

As part of my professional portfolio, I need to demonstrate that my students are learning the skills that I am teaching. To do this, I would like to use your student's work as part of my evidence to show my growth as an educator. All names and identifying marks will be removed so that anyone who looks at my portfolio will see only the student's work. I would appreciate your help by giving your permission for me use a copy of:

_____

_____.

    If you have any questions or concerns, please do not hesitate to call me. Thank you for helping me achieve my goal of becoming a stronger educator!

I release my child's work for submission in the teaching portfolio.

_____
Parent/Guardian signature

I do not release my child's work for the teaching portfolio.

_____
Parent/Guardian signature

Dear Parent/Guardian,

As part of my professional portfolio, I need to demonstrate that my students are learning the skills that I am teaching. To show my evidence, I would like to include a photo of the class at work as part of my portfolio. No names will be used so that students remain anonymous to anyone who looks at my portfolio. I would appreciate your help by giving your permission for me to use a photo of our class and/or your child individually.

    If you have any questions or concerns, please do not hesitate to call me. Thank you for helping me achieve my goal of becoming an outstanding educator!

I release my child's photo for submission in the teaching portfolio.

_____
Parent/Guardian signature

I do not release my child's photo for the teaching portfolio.

_____
Parent/Guardian signature

MODIFICATIONS FOR SPECIAL NEEDS

preferential seating

dictation

oral tests & assignments

technology

calculators

word processors

choices

multiple choice spelling tests

literature response journals

alternate forms of work

talk directly to students
   with hearing impairments

overheads & other visual aids

reduce size of task

larger print

work in pairs or groups

manipulatives

extra time

hands-on activities

mixed groups

change materials to fit goals

offer challenges at all levels

variety of assessment tools

pretests

role-plays

students tape record answers

books printed in Braille

Teaching English-Language Learners: 10 Tips

1. It is imperative that teachers form positive, caring relationships with their students. This is the key to becoming a successful teacher. Find out about your students' lives; connect with them; tell them about your life. Ask them what they're going to do on the weekend. Tell them stories. Show them pictures of your family. If students feel cared about and feel that you have a genuine interest in who they are, then they will be invested in the learning process. School will become more meaningful to them, and this can only enhance learning.

2. Create a learning atmosphere that is open and tolerant; one that not only recognizes diversity, but celebrates it. Do not establish a punitive environment in which students are prevented from communicating in their native language. Remember that language is closely related to identity. Language learning is a very complicated process; the learning of academic language is even more challenging when hindered by the schools' subtractive devaluing of non-native students' language.

3. Use a "Country of the Month" bulletin board to highlight the countries and cultures of each of your students. Assign a different topic for each student to research (e.g., art, music, history, map and flag, holidays, language, etc.). This is a great way for teachers to tap into the great wealth of diversity and cultural knowledge that students have. It is also a great way to connect students' backgrounds with academic content to make for a more meaningful school experience.

4. Play games! Scrabble, Scattegories, and Vocabulary Bingo are perfect for English-language learning.

5. Be their advocate. Make sure they are getting the kind of support that they need in their mainstream classes so that they don't fall through the cracks. Collaborate with mainstream teachers. Modify tests. Create study guides. Make flash cards. Build background knowledge.

6. Display student work. Don't let there be any white space on your classroom walls. Show off the great work they've done! Also, keep examples of your students' best work. When you assign the project next year, you will have a benchmark to show your students.

7. Keep portfolios. This is a great way to compile data and demonstrate growth. Have students fold a sheet of construction paper in half and decorate the covers. Students should keep their best work in their portfolios, plus all tests, quizzes, and papers. When parents come, you will have something ready to show them.

8. Have high expectations, and do not accept anything less. Students will rise to the occasion if you believe in them. You'll be amazed at how much language a young person can acquire in just a short amount of time. English-language learners need support, but they don't need to be coddled. Because they are acquiring a new language as well as content, they need to work extra hard.

9. Be flexible. You will constantly need to assess and adjust accordingly. Always check for understanding. If they're not getting it, it's your fault! Always be ready to change your lesson plan, if necessary.

10. Be enthusiastic. If you think it's boring, how do you think they feel? Think of new and interesting ways to present material. Break the mold. Surprise them! Be creative, and have fun.

State Education and Certification Offices

Alabama Dept. of Education
Gordon Persons Office Bldg.
50 N. Ripley St.
Montgomery, AL 36130-3901
(205) 242-9977
http://www.alsde.edu

Alaska Dept. of Education
P.O. Box F
801 W. 10th St., Ste. 200
Juneau, AK 99801-1894
(907) 465-2810
http://www.educ.state.ak.us

Arizona Dept. of Public
Instruction
P.O. Box 25609
1535 W. Jefferson
Phoenix, AZ 85002
(602) 542-4368
http://ade.state.az.us

Arkansas Dept. of Education
4 State Capitol Mall
Little Rock, AR 72201-1071
(501) 682-4342
http://arkedu.ik12.ar.us/

California Dept. of Education
721 Capitol Mall
Sacramento, CA 95814
(916) 657-5485
http://goldmine.cde.ca.gov

Colorado Dept. of Education
210 E. Colfax Ave.
Denver, CO 80203
(303) 866-6628
http://www.cde.state.co.us

Connecticut Dept. of Education
P.O. Box 2219
Hartford, CT 06145-2219
(203) 566-5201
http://www.aces.k12.ct.
us/csdf

Delaware Dept. of Public
Instruction
P.O. Box 1402,
Townsend Bldg. #279
Federal and Lockeman Streets
Dover, DE 19903
(302) 739-4688
http://www.dpi.state.de.us

District of Columbia, Division
of State Services Teacher
Education
415 12th St. NW, Room 1013
Washington, DC 20004
(202) 724-4246
http://www.k12.dc.us

Florida Dept. of Education
Room PL 08, Capitol Bldg.
Tallahassee, FL 32301
(904) 487-1785
http://www.firn.edu/doe

Georgia Dept. of Education
2066 Twin Towers East
Atlanta, GA 30334-5020
(404) 657-9000
http://www.doe.k12.ga.us

Hawaii Dept. of Education
P.O. Box 2360
Honolulu, HI 96804
(808) 586-3420
http://www.K12.hi.us

Idaho Dept. of Education
L.B. Jordan Office Bldg.
650 W. State St.
Boise, ID 83720-3650
http://www.sde.state.id.us

Illinois Board of Education
100 N. 1st St.
Springfield, IL 62777
(217) 782-4321
http://www.isbe.state.il.us

Indiana Dept. of Education
Room 229, State House
Indianapolis, IN 46204-2798
(317) 232-6665
http://www.doe.state.in.us

Iowa Dept. of Education
Grimes State Office Bldg.
East 14th and Grand Streets
Des Moines, IA 50319-0147
(515) 281-3245
http://www.state.ia.us/educate

Kansas Dept. of Education
Kansas State Education Bldg.
120 E. 10th St.
Topeka, KS 66612-1182
(913) 296-2288
http://www.ksbe.state.ks.us

Kentucky Dept. of Education
18th Floor, Capital Plaza Tower
500 Mero St.
Frankfort, KY 40601
(502) 564-4606
http://www.kde.state.ky.us

Louisiana Dept. of Education
P.O. Box 94064
Baton Rouge, LA 70804-9064
(504) 342-3490
http://www.doe.state.la.us

Maine Dept. of Education
State House Station 23
Augusta, ME 04333
(207) 287-5944
http://www.state.me.us/
education/homepage.htm

Maryland Dept. of Education
200 W. Baltimore St.
Baltimore, MD 20201
(301) 333-2142
http://sailor.lib.md.us/msde

Michigan Dept. of Education
P.O. Box 30008
Lansing, MI 48909
(517) 373-3310
http://www.mde.state.mi.us

Minnesota Dept. of Education
616 Capitol Square Bldg.
St. Paul, MN 55101
(612) 296-2046
http://www.educ.state.mn.us

Mississippi Dept. of Education
P.O. Box 771
550 High St.
Jackson, MS 39205-0771
(601) 359-3483
http://mdek12.state.ms.us

Missouri Dept. of Elementary
and Secondary Education
P.O. Box 480
205 Jefferson St.
Jefferson City, MO 65102
(314) 751-0051
http://services.dese.state.mo.us

Montana Office of Public
Instruction
P.O. Box 202501
106 State Capitol
Helena, MT 59620-2501
(406) 444-3150
http://161.7.114.15/OPI/
OPIHTML

Nebraska Dept. of Education
301 Centennial Mall South
P.O. Box 94987
Lincoln, NE 68509-4987
(800) 371-4642
http://www.NDE.State.NE.US

Nevada Dept. of Education
1850 E. Sahara, Ste. 200
Las Vegas, NV 89158
(702) 386-5401
http://www.state.nv.us/

New Hampshire Dept. of
Education
101 Pleasant St., State Office
Park South
Concord, NH 03301
(603) 271-2407
http://www.state.nh.us/doe/
education.html

New Jersey Dept. of Education
CN 503
Trenton, NJ 08625-0503
(609) 292-2070
http://www.state.nj.us/education

New Mexico Dept. of Education
Education Bldg.
300 Don Gaspar
Santa Fe, NM 87501-2786
(505) 827-6587
http://sde.state.nm.us

New York Office of Teaching
Room 5A11-CEC
State Education Dept.
Albany, NY 12230
(518) 474-3901
http://www.nysed.gov

North Carolina Dept. of Public
Instruction
301 N. Wilmington St.
Raleigh, NC 27601-2825
(919) 733-4125
http://www.dpi.state.nc.us

North Dakota Dept. of Public
Instruction
State Capitol Bldg., 11th Floor
600 Boulevard Ave. E.
Bismarck, ND 58505-0440
(701) 224-2264
http://www.sendit.nodak.edu/
dpi

Ohio Dept. of Education
65 S. Front St., Rm. 1012
Columbus, OH 43266-0308
(614) 466-3593
http://www.ode.ohio.gov

Oklahoma Professional
Standards
Dept. of Education
Oliver Hodge Memorial
Education Bldg.
2500 N. Lincoln Blvd.
Rm. 211
Oklahoma City, OK 73105-4599
(405) 521-3337
http://www.sde.state.ok.us

Oregon Dept. of Education
700 Pringle Pkwy. SE
Salem, OR 97310-0290
(503) 378-3573
http://www.state.or.us

Pennsylvania Dept. of
Education
333 Market St., 10th Floor
Harrisburg, PA 17126-0333
(717) 787-2967
http://www.cas.psu.edu/
pde.html

Rhode Island Dept. of
Education
22 Hayes St.
Providence, RI 02908
(401) 277-2675
http://instruct.ride.ri.net/

South Carolina Dept. of
Education
10006 Rutledge Bldg.
1429 Senate St.
Columbia, SC 29201
(803) 734-8492
http://www.state.sc.us/sde

South Dakota Teacher
Education and Certification
Dept. of Education
700 Governors Dr.
Pierre, SD 57501-2291
(605) 773-3553
http://www.state.sd.us

Tennessee Dept. of Education
100 Cordell Hull Bldg.
Nashville, TN 37243-0375
(615) 741-2731
http://www.state.tn.us

Texas Education Agency
William B. Travis Bldg.
1701 N. Congress Ave.
Austin, TX 78701-1494
(512) 463-8976
http://www.tea.texas.gov

Utah Office of Education
250 E. 500 South St.
Salt Lake City, UT 84111
(801) 538-7740
http://www.usoe.k12.ut.us

Vermont Dept. of Education
120 State St.
Montpelier, VT 05602-2703
(802) 828-2445
http://www.state.vt.us/educ

Virginia Dept. of Education
James Monroe Bldg.
Fourteenth & Franklin Streets
P.O. Box 6-Q
Richmond, VA 23216-2120
(804) 225-2755
http://www.pen.k12.va.us

Washington Dept. of Public
Instruction
Old Capitol Bldg.
P.O. Box 47200
Olympia, WA 98504-7200
(206) 753-6773
http://www.ospi.wednet.edu

West Virginia Dept. of
Education
Bldg. 6, Room 337
1900 Kanawha Blvd. E.
Charleston, WV 25305-0330
(800) 982-2378
http://access.k12.wv.us

Wisconsin Dept. of Public
Instruction
P.O. Box 7841
125 S. Webster St.
Madison, WI 53707-7841
(608) 266-1027
http://badger.state.wi.us/
agencies/dpi

Wyoming Dept. of Education
2300 Capitol Ave.
Hathaway Bldg., 2nd Floor
Cheyenne, WY 82002
(307) 777-7291
http://www.k12.wy.us

Suggested Table of Contents Based on INTASC

I. Standard: Knowledge of Subject

  A. Record of courses
  B. Practicum/Clinical experience
  C. Research papers
  D. Certificates of completion of workshops
  E. Summaries of related articles
  F. Bibliography of related texts

II. Standard: Learning and Human Development

  A. Sample lesson plans created for a variety of age groups
  B. Reflections on the difference between your 2nd-grade clinical students and your 6th-grade clinical students
  C. A bibliography of children's books with suggestions for age-appropriateness
  D. Term paper comparing and contrasting the theories of renowned child psychologists

III. Standard: Adapting Instruction

  A. Group project completed in your mainstreaming class
  B. Descriptions of curricular modifications you've tried and their outcomes
  C. Reflection on the role you played in an IEP meeting
  D. Letter from parents thanking you for the extra time you put into modifying the social studies test for their child with learning disabilities
  E. Examples of how you make curriculum more challenging for students with gifted abilities
  F. Narrative paper on your decision-making process when creating lesson plans to include students with English as a second language

IV. Standard: Strategies

  A. Video of you teaching a lesson
  B. Self-evaluation identifying methods you've found success with and others that still need work
  C. Narrative descriptions of the methods used by your cooperating teachers
  D. Research project on the battles of controversy between experts in the field of classroom instruction
  E. Rationale for changing cooperative learning groups before midsemester

V. Standard: Motivation and Classroom Management

  A. Letters home updating parents on coming projects and homework
  B. Examples of certificates you've created for achievements such as:
    1. improved behavior
    2. excellent effort

      3. all homework in on time for the month

      4. improved attendance

  C. Copy of classroom assertive discipline plan, including:

      1. rules

      2. consequences

      3. student/teacher-generated reward system

      4. charts

  D. Certificate of completion of special classroom management course, seminar, or workshop

  E. Letters of appreciation from parents grateful for the extra effort you gave to their child with emotional or behavioral problems

  F. Summaries of articles on classroom management and/or motivation

VI. Standard: Communication Skills

  A. Letter to parents introducing yourself as student teacher

  B. Copies of minutes from team meetings showing your participation

  C. Copies of position or persuasive papers you've written

  D. Copies of group projects you've completed, demonstrating your ability to work in a group

  E. Certificates of your technological abilities, including:

      1. word processing

      2. Internet

      3. database

      4. spreadsheets

      5. hyperlinks

      6. digital cameras

      7. scanners

  F. Address of your Web site with hard copies of documents included there

  G. Samples of your best handwriting in a handwritten essay (many districts require this in their employment applications)

  H. A video of you presenting a lesson to a class

  I. PowerPoint presentation of your philosophy of teaching

VII. Standard: Planning

  A. Copies of lesson plans from each subject and grade level you've worked with differs

  B. Copies of curriculum you've created

  C. Copies of group presentations you've team-taught in your courses

  D. A schedule of the entire school day from your clinical experience

  E. Examples of seating charts you've designed

  F. Scope and sequence of a unit you wish to teach

VIII. Standard: Assessment

  A. Copies of established informal assessment charts you've used, citing authors

  B. Copies of informal assessments you've created, including your rationale

C. Copies of objective tests you've created
D. Examples of how you modify assessments for students with special learning needs
E. Skill inventories you've used or would like to use
F. Learning modality inventories you've learned how to use
G. Summaries of articles on multiple intelligences
H. Papers you've written on multicultural issues in assessment

IX. Standard: Commitment

A. Your statement of beliefs/philosophy of education
B. Certificates of participation in community events
C. Articles about your volunteer work with nonprofit groups
D. Your résumé, focusing on the time you've spent working with children in and out of the school setting

X. Standard: Partnerships

A. Documentation of the help you provided to coordinate a community volunteer drive for your local public school system
B. Your written thoughts on a legislative session you attended in your state's capital when they discussed education issues
C. Letters from your local legislators thanking you for meeting with them to discuss education issues
D. Minutes from the school board meeting you attended to observe how their decision-making process works
E. Letters from a parent/teacher organization thanking you for your help
F. Letters you've written to local businesses suggesting ways that they can participate to help improve public education in your town

Index